BORN GIFTED

*How to Unwrap the Gifts Inside
You for Supernatural Success!*

NISAN TROTTER

ISBN 978-1-64114-050-8 (paperback)
ISBN 978-1-64114-052-2 (hardcover)
ISBN 978-1-64114-051-5 (digital)

Christian Faith Publishing, Inc.
832 Park Avenue
Meadville, PA 16335
www.christianfaithpublishing.com

Edited by: Mavian Arocha-Rowe
Cover Design by: Sharee Faircloth

Printed in the United States of America

Dedication

To be writing the dedication page of my first book is mind-blowing.

First, thank God for Jesus, who knew I would write Born Gifted before time began. May this work make you smile and throw a block party for the angels in heaven.

Wepa! To my lovely wife, Yorelis, who stands in unending support of every endeavor, you make my heart sing. I know you love my "cheesy" because it's sharper than Kraft. Thank you for tirelessly watching the boys while I worked feverishly on *Born Gifted*. Thank you for listening to me read many lines of this book out loud and checking to make sure my thoughts were coherent. I owe you nothing but love. My love is a debt that will forever remain outstanding.

To my handsome, curly-haired boys, Onesimus and Osias, by the time you are old enough to read and understand, I pray *Born Gifted* has touched the lives of countless. Then when desire leads you to turning the pages of my book, do realize how blessed I am to be your papi. Easily, you two are my favorites! I pray you two far exceed everything I've accomplished on earth with God's grace minus the pressure and stress.

To Marilyn Coats (my amazing mother and African American queen), in every day committed to writing, I thought about how proud you were of my efforts. It fueled me to finish because we made a verbal agreement when I was a child to "never give up!" Life will get even sweeter. Keep fighting, Mom.

I owe thanks to so many people for their love, support, and motivation. You've helped shape my journey in life to be nothing short of special. You know exactly who you are and why you mean so much to me. You will not take offense that your name isn't included in the dedication because of knowing your name is inscribed on my heart. I love you. This book is dedicated to you too!

Contents

Preface 7

1.   The Three Fs...9

2.   No More Boredom..16

3.   You're a Natural..21

4.   The Irrevocable Gifts...26

5.   Talent Advisory Alert..30

6.   Read the Context Clues....................................38

7.   Friction 44

8.   Mac-and-Cheese Greatness.............................51

9.   Character > Gift..57

10. I Quit..63

11. Move Over. My Gift Is Too Big! 71

12. Fulfill Your Assignment 77

13. It's a War Zone 83

14. Work Your Gift 89

15. Live Creative 96

16. Gift Restoration 102

17. A Difference in Belief......................................106

18. Amazing Grace..115

Epilogue..121

Your Personal Invitation 125

Preface

Hi, I'm Nisan Trotter. Yep! Nisan. Just like the car, minus one *s*. This is how I introduce myself to strangers, but they often look at me cross-eyed as if I don't know my name. Whether it's the customer service representative who gets it wrong or the barista who yells my order ("Number 8...Nye-saan"), I generally smirk and gently correct, "It's Nisan. Just like the car, minus one *s*."

Now that we have cleared the first point of order, let me express the pure excitement of being in your presence. Each time you pick up a book and start reading it, you're spending time with that book's author; I don't take this moment for granted. Because you are the proud owner of *Born Gifted*, let's consider ourselves strategic partners on a fantastic voyage. By the time you and I complete (key word: *complete*) our navigation through this book, your level of maturity will be deeper than the wavy blue seas.

You see, I'm a firm believer in the following: As I grow, the people in my circle grow.

You motivated me to do and be more. I literally had you in mind while writing every line of *Born Gifted*. Why? Because I want to see the absolute best revealed in you. My desire is to receive a testimonial back from you saying something like "Nisan, your book was life changing for me. I feel so alive because of your words!"

No longer could I ignore the burning desire to share some of my best life stories, crafty self-help content, and passionate coaching. You are in my sphere of influence now, and it is my God-given responsibility to encourage, inspire, motivate, and challenge you. If I do not follow through on the aforementioned, then I have failed you. And I'm not going to fail. My confidence is sky-high because God put me in a headlock and He wouldn't let go until I completed *Born Gifted*.

Who am I? I'm the author of *Born Gifted*, an inspirational book I wrote from the depths of my heart; the husband of a beautiful Puerto Rican queen named Yorelis; the daddy of two rambunctious boys, Onesimus and Osias; a fitness entrepreneur dubbed the Fitness Preacher among the sainted in the fitness industry; a homeowner whose childhood family of four grew up in the back bedroom of Grandmomma's house; a former competitive collegiate football player at the prestigious Bucknell University (ray Bucknell!) child of the Most High God and so much more!

Born Gifted is not about me or my accolades. It's about you, your quest to discover what you were born to do, and how to accelerate and excel.

So I triple-dog-dare you to open your heart and mind to the words I've written, from start to finish. I vow: there is no way you will remain the same upon completion.

Chapter 1

THE THREE *F*s

Feed your fears and your faith will starve.
Feed your faith, and your fears will.

—Max Lucado

Allow me to teach you about the three *F*s: fear, failure, and future. These three words are powerfully interconnected and necessary to discuss. I want you to revisit the three *F*s with every fill in the blank and challenge located at the end of each chapter. When doing so, ask yourself the following question: do I feel fear, forecast failure, or fret about my future as I close out the chapter? Why this question? I want you to be in tune with your emotions throughout the entire book and journal when needed.

Allow me to provide some examples of how the three *F*s showed up in my life. You will gain valuable insight on how to use my stories to unlock your supernatural gifts.

First, let's discuss fear.

Anything big enough will scare you. Brahma bulls, great white sharks, polar bears, and safari lions are mammoth-size animals. Having a healthy fear of them is wisdom at work. You do not see long lines of people waiting to pet these creatures, right? Well, whenever we approach certain situations in life, which project our success, it's very easy to treat them like some of the world's most dangerous animals. The illusion of our head being gnawed off is forecast. This fear stops us dead in our tracks as opposed to inspiring us to take steps forward. Might I suggest, unless you are in the vicinity of a tiger shark or something of the like, that you move forward. Do the opposite of what you are feeling when approaching enormous goals, ambitions, and dreams. Naturally, you will want to freeze or even retreat when fear rises in your heart. But taking action gives fear a kidney punch. Move forward in the face of fear. Stare it in the eyeball, and walk in its direction. And take note: fear may appear gigantic from afar, but as you make progress, it will minimize.

I recall freezing on the football field when an angry big, 250-pound lineman came running in my direction. Because I was a small kid who perhaps looked a hair bigger in full pads, my thoughts sounded like this: *They're going to swallow me for lunch!* The fear of hard tackles made me quit my seventh-grade football team. Do you see how fear leads to failure, which ultimately impacted my future?

I never considered myself a failure or a quitter, but I allowed fear to get in my way from something I loved. I loved the game. I loved competing. I loved putting on my decorated jersey. But I hated the arousal of fear when I thought about the pulverizing hits. I became a little scaredy-cat, and this led me straight off the squad.

My future in the sport of football looked grim; however, by junior high school, my best friend, Edric Prim, talked me into giving the sport another shot. It was then when I discovered, if I simply kept moving and imposed my speed on the game, my fear would settle and devastating tackles could be avoided. So I ran. In fact, I ran like a chicken toward the end zone. And it worked beautifully! Do you see the message within the message? You can run like a chicken as long as you're headed in the right direction! Whenever the bigger-than-you obstacles approach, move. Run scared if you have to. And as long as you are running forward, you will be okay. No more retreating.

As I moved and made a name for myself on the gridiron, a $160,000 scholarship to play college football knocked on my door. I gladly answered and said, "Come to Papa!"

I want you to remember the first *F* when reading through *Born Gifted*. It's an important one to have victory over. Be on guard. When you beat fear the first time, it will come back in another shape, form, or fashion. However, you will be ready because you know the cure. My high-priced scholarship meant frequent-flier miles up north to play ball in Lewisburg, Pennsylvania. As a sweet Southern boy from Alabama, I was afraid of heights, especially flying. Fear asked for another dance. This time, I was ready to tango because the same blow that knocked it out the first time knocked it out again. I took action (kidney punch) and stepped onto the plane toward my destiny. As you overcome fear, your confidence builds to conquer your next battle with it. Warning: You are going to read some scary big advice from me in the coming chapters. Use my prescription for success when handling fear. Do like the chorus in Erick Morillo's hit song "I like to Move It."

The second *F* is for *failure*.

Failure is not failure. Failure is an opportunity to grow. Failure is a chance to get better. Failure has the power to teach great lessons if you pay attention; if you are willing to reflect and make adjustments. Is failure enjoyable? No. Does it hurt? Absolutely.

I will confess, I am not the best at numbers and calculations. One time, I scored a whopping 7 on my math exam in school. That's right. A 7. If there was any letter more suitable than an *F* to represent failure, then I would have earned it too. The score I received was so embarrassing. You're probably thinking I scored poorly because of my lack of study, however, that is far from the truth. You see, I worked my butt off to grade out at a 7. So what happens when you give it your absolute best and still fail? You keep trying. You keep pressing on. You have mental resiliency. Moving forward, I worked longer and harder at math, got a tutor, and made this subject submit to my willpower. I did not become an A+ student, but I learned what I could and survived the class.

Ironically, for my first job out of college, I was financial advisor for one of the most prominent investment firms in Pensacola, Florida (about forty-five minutes away from my hometown in Silverhill, Alabama). Who would have imagined a poor math student alive in an environment where stocks and bonds traveled? Before officially becoming a broker, I needed to pass the Series 7. No pun intended to go from making a 7 on my math exam to having to pass a broker's exam named the Series 7. It's synonymous to the bar exam lawyers take before practicing in their field. I'm certain it's not as difficult, but it was hard enough for me. The 7 is a rite of passage to play with people's money. More numbers and fancy calculations found themselves back in my life. However, because of my first failure in math, I knew exactly what to do when the going got tough in preparation for test day—I kept trying, kept putting in the effort, and had the mindset to make this exam part of my legacy. I failed practice test after practice test, but I refused to give up. On the sit-in day for the exam, I passed by the hair on my chinny chin chin. That was the easy part. Apparently, trying to get high-net-worth clients to invest millions of dollars with you was much more difficult.

I traveled near and far along the roads of Pensacola, spending precious gas and meal money, to treat some of the most successful in the area to breakfast, brunch, lunch, snacks, dinner, and so forth. I collected newspapers, searched the yellow pages, joined the local chamber, and asked around to know the who's who of the area. My pitch to get in front of them was simple but effective: "Hi, my name is Nisan Trotter, new financial adviser at XYZ. May I treat you to lunch in exchange for some advice?" Meeting often with a bunch of high-net-worth people made me feel low and broke because I never walked away with them as my clients. They were willing to give me advice but not their money. I was told no more times than Steve Urkel when he asked Laura Winslow out for a date from *Family Matters* (a popular sitcom that aired in the eighties and nineties).

Never landing the big account led to a day I remember crystal clear, even though it was over a decade ago.

I arrived to work like any other morning, except this time, I got called into the branch manager's office.

"Nisan."

"Yes, sir?"

"Today will be your last day."

Wow. Within a twinkling of an eye, I was fired. I was fired so fast I didn't even realize what happened. My assistant was waiting outside of the manager's office door to immediately escort me out the building. I couldn't collect any key contacts I made, only my personal belongings, and out the back door I went. I failed, or so I thought.

Question: "Have you ever felt good about being fired?"

At first, it stung when this premier financial shop (everyone knew of) asked me to leave the premises immediately for not meeting quota (although I tried my hardest). They made my assistant walk me out the back door. Yet before I could even arrive home, I was praising God because I hated this job. Something really bad happened to me, something that makes folks have a nervous breakdown; however, I was breaking out in songs of praise. I was still alive. I still had a chance to make it. I figured it could have been worse.

The lessons I learned from my brief stint working as an FA still resonate with me today. Here are five of them:

1. Never take anything for granted because things can change in a flash; stay appreciative.
2. Even in the middle of some of your toughest storms, you can still smile.
3. Failure is not a person. It's a growth opportunity to learn valuable lessons.
4. Nearly anyone (even the who's who) will meet with you when genuinely asking them for advice.
5. Stay humble without harboring feelings of bitterness toward others, those on top, those who assist, and those who sit in the bull pen with you.

Open your ears to failure's voice. It has a sound. Actually, failure is surprisingly talkative and more helpful than harmful. As you continue reading *Born Gifted*, you may be reminded of some of your mistakes, mishaps, and failures. Use these moments as leverage for your future.

The third *F* is *future*.

Your future hangs in the balance between freezing in fear and not learning from failure. Life is unpredictable. Adjustments constantly need to be made, and many times you have to be flexible and make changes on the fly. One good or bad phone call, text message, or e-mail can alter your life plans. In other words, you have to be ready for the unexpected.

When the unexpected "fire Nisan" scenario took place, it was both shocking and humiliating. Brokers in the bull pen next to me stared in fear, for themselves, as I packed my stuff and walked out the back door. I could have folded or curled up in a ball. I could have sung a sad song with the violin playing in the background. Instead, I kept telling myself, "You've been through tougher times, Nisan. It's going to be okay. God's got you!" I immediately recognized my unforeseen strength to keep moving and keep my head held high. It was time to start working on the next game plan. No time for whining, and I needed to act fast.

With little money in my pocket and the bank account dwindling away, with limited options of employment in a small hometown, my future was scary. After taking a deep breath and quickly pressing Reset, I reached out to my Uncle Clifford, who built fences in the nearly unbearable heat of Alabama.

I had (and still have) tons of respect for Uncle Clifford. He is a guy who does not complain. He simply straps up the steel-toe boots and works his butt off.

Like Uncle Clifford, I wasn't afraid of work either, so I asked him for a job. I told him I would be a good worker and do anything he asked. He saved me. He brought me on board, and I went from white-collar to blue-collar in a flash. It paid the bills. Plus, I got to see how cool my uncle was because we spent lots of time together.

I will never forget studying the technical analytic stock trends on my desktop in air-conditioning. Then in an instant, I was slamming a posthole digger into the ground (under the Alabama heat) to dig fence holes for my uncle, now new boss. With a $160,000 education at hand, life changed quickly.

The lesson learned: Failure doesn't mean death. In order to make it to a bright future, you have to sometimes roll up your sleeves, turn on survival mode, get down and dirty, and body slam the unpredictable life we live.

A favorite quote from my mother is "Son, do what you gotta do until you can do what you wanna do!"

Is this the future I had planned, tacking up fence boards? Nothing wrong with it, but is it wrong for me? Is this the end of the road where the bus stops? Could I survive and weather this storm? I've dealt with fear before. I've failed before. Now I'm here sweating in the heat and concerned about where I'm headed.

My dream was to be a business owner of some sort, to demonstrate that entrepreneur's edge everyone around me admired. I wanted to help countless people. I simply did not imagine fence work as a part of the equation. At this moment in time, my only hope of arriving to my destiny was to keep digging deep. So that's what I did. I dug and dug and dug some more.

I don't want you (for a second) to discount the grand future that lies ahead because of fears and failures. Recount the three *F*s (fear, failure, and future) often from day to day and recognize their connection for your advancement.

Born Gifted is designed for anyone who has goals, dreams, and ambitions to conquer. It reveals why you have a supernatural gifting in you to accelerate and excel. You will soon feel empowered to unwrap your special gifts and talents, plus achieve a life of success by playing the unique role God designed for you at birth.

Chapter 2

NO MORE BOREDOM

Life is either a daring adventure
or nothing at all.

—Helen Keller

God would never create you for the purpose of boredom. We don't have a Maker who gets pleasure in the twiddling of our thumbs, whining, and complaining about nothing to do on earth. He spent a lot of time and hard work creating the sun, moon, stars, green grass, and beautiful flowers. I, for one, believe He spent even more time uniquely creating you, me, and the billions of others around us. Nobody is the same.

Think about the level of creative thought put into ensuring there isn't even the same set of fingerprints. There are countless originally shaped ears, eyes, and noses. Wrinkles on the forehead, hairy toes, vibrant smiles—it all varies from one person to the next. Our bodies are designed like nobody else, and imagine, I'm only referring to physical features. Where do I begin in discussing the vast differences among us emotionally, mentally, and spiritually? It's mind-boggling! Psalms 139:13–14 says, "You alone created my inner being. You knitted me together inside my mother. I will give thanks to you because I have been so amazingly and miraculously made [GWT]." Wow…

Psalms 139:15 continues with "[He] skillfully made you in the secret place." I picture Him in the heavenly, majestic laboratory creating us in ways only a sovereign mind could. He reached into the vast depth of His genius, navigated through the channels of His larger-than-life vision to singularly create you and me. Please start feeling good or at least better right now, my friend. Christmas has now been introduced to you in a brand-new way. I'm not referring to ornaments on the pine. There will not be a serenade of "Jingle Bells" or "Rudolph, the Red-Nosed Reindeer" at this juncture. It's time for you to unwrap gifts, very big gifts.

God is no respecter of persons (Romans 2:11), meaning He does not play favoritism. He reigns over the just as well as the unjust. He is so good we cannot even fathom. Unmerited gifts are given to both the good and the bad. You have your gifts, and I have mine. Therefore, some very necessary unwrapping must take place. Inside of you are custom-made gifts from your Creator. The One who gave the sun its home in the sky, the One who told the seas they can only go so far, the One who mapped out land's territory has also placed qualities, attributes, talents, abilities, and gifts in you.

Upon opening your gift, the real fun begins. How ludicrous would it be if we kept gifts in their wrapping paper? As a parent of two boys, I absolutely love to see the delight on their faces when it's time to shred through gift wrapping. They dismantle cardboard boxes like dogs with clenched jaws shaking their heads violently. They are eager to see what's inside. And with joy, I'm nearly foaming at the mouth because my heart is swelling for their ecstasy. In such a case, God is no different, and we should be like my boys every time Papi brings home a gift.

You get to use God-given gifts to have fun, explore, serve man-kind, and live in massive success. Prosperity is in your gift. The misty black cloud of boredom hanging over your head now vanishes into thin air because you are doing what you are born to do with your gift. Get excited for a fantastic adventure. The nature of this thrill isn't going to last a few minutes like a roller-coaster ride or a cup of vanilla bean ice cream (my wife's favorite). Once you discover what God has implanted in you, get ready for an everlasting journey of euphoria with your gift. Picture it as an ever-present bond—meant to make you happy, excited about life, and ready to take on each day with passion and fervor.

If you show me a person dissatisfied with life, then I will demonstrate how this person is detached from their gifting. How can real joy take place in a person's life when they aren't using what God has graciously given for joy and success? How can you play at a world-class level without knowing your unique talents and abilities?

Imagine if Walt Disney tried to specialize in computer programming. Imagine if twenty-three-time gold medalist Michael Phelps traded in his Speedos for nicely creased slacks to work in corporate America. Imagine if Maya Angelou stopped pulling on heartstrings with her beautiful poetry to be a weathercaster. It does not make sense. Sounds weird, right? Given we know how much Walt Disney means to animated film, given we know Michael Phelps' gigantic contribution to the Olympic Games, given we know Maya Angelou's penmanship to lyrical truths, it seems preposterous to view them in any other place than where they're currently cemented in history. They nailed their purpose by flourishing in their gift. If you want a recipe made of frustration, jealousy, envy, and boredom, then abandon your gift.

When you figure out what you were born to do and use your supernatural gifts to execute God's game plan, get ready to score big.

I played wide receiver for the Orange and Blue, Bucknell University, Bison Football Team. Some of the best moments of my life happened on the 120-yard gridiron. Still to this very day, over a decade later, I remember the two touchdown grabs hauled in when we played Columbia University's Lions. Oh, t'was was a glorious feat! My team won the game sizably, 42–16 ('ray Bucknell!). Indeed, the Patriot League and Ivy League are archrivals. It's been so for centuries.

On September 25, 2004, the Bison Football Team got the better of the Lions. It was a balmy summer night in front of 8,233 fans, and I was having the time of my life. Was it the cheerleaders leading the crowds? Was it the band playing our fight song? Was it strategizing and giving our all under the bright lights? Sure! In part, each played a role and had their impact on my happiness, but the real reason for jubilee was my gift operating in beast mode. I was given an opportunity to do what I was born to do. God blessed me with athletic abilities like catching the football and running very elusively to avoid scary tackles by the opposition (even though I did sustain a mild cushion in an intrasquad game, but we won't talk about this). I knew my role on the team and practiced my craft religiously, leading up to catching not one but two long touchdown passes against Columbia. The countless ball-catching drills, wind sprints, route running, and hours in the playbook enabled me to lead my team to a sweet victory.

I never felt so acrobatic than when dire circumstances called for me to stretch out for a diving catch in the back of the end zone. My gift shined brightest, seemingly out of nowhere. I flew like a stealth bomber for a split second to make the grab and then immediately found myself in a swarm of teammates cheering me on.

Do you think I was bored? Of course not. Every sense in my body was awakened. I felt alive! My gift swooped in to save the day. Today, I have lasting memories to cherish and share with my two boys over and over again, or at least until they say, "Pops, we've heard this story a thousand times! Enough!"

God doesn't want you to waste precious time. Actually, not another second should be spent without you acknowledging your gift. I'm here to help you discover the greatness within. It must come out. No more hitting the snooze button. Time-out for punching the clock, only to exist like a walking zombie at an unfulfilling job. It's time to jump out of bed with enthusiasm; no alarm clock required. Your passion will now wake the rooster up.

You will have a zeal for life because of the opportunity to use your God-given powers. Resist the plight of those who choose to sit on the sideline, acting as if they are giftless. You will no longer be dull to the world, restricted by the same boring daily routines. Nope. Not during or after reading *Born Gifted*. We will leave bran-cereal Mondays, computer-gazing Tuesdays, plop-on-the-sofa Wednesdays, channel-surfing Thursdays, and frozen-pizza Fridays to someone else. As for you and me, we will gladly use our God-given gifts to make every day feel like the weekend.

Fill in the Blanks

1. If you show me a person dissatisfied with life, then I will demonstrate how this person is _____ from their gift.

2. God is no _____ of persons, meaning He doesn't play _____.

3. Resist the plight of those who choose to sit on the sideline, acting as if they are _____.

Chapter Challenge

Never say you are bored again! Find something cool to do with your gift.

Chapter 3

YOU'RE A NATURAL

Being a singer is a natural gift. It means,
I'm using to the highest degree possible, the gift
that God gave me to use. I'm happy with that.

—Aretha Franklin

Don't worry! I know what you're thinking. After reading chapter 2, your thoughts are now jumbled. Everything inside you screams, "Yes! He's right. I was created to live large and in charge with my God-given gifts." However, you're also wondering if my proclamation is a fairy tale absent of the truth. Are you struggling to believe with the utmost depth? May I advise that soaring is not only for the eagles, my friend? You may have missed the memo regarding the power of your gifts, but you will now have the remedy for on-time arrival with God's best for you. Hang on. You are going to beat the clock with time to spare.

First, the dreamer inside you must never die. As a kid, your dreams and beliefs were more precious than gold. You believed in the tooth fairy, Santa Claus, and the Easter bunny, remember? Your faith was classified as both unshakeable and innocent. How dare anyone try to deter you from your convictions as a youngster. You would look at naysayers with an awkward stare for their disbelief. You believed in superheroes and magic, which is why cartoons were so fascinating. Flying wasn't a far-fetched idea either. If your role model said, "You can jump over a building like Superman in one single bound." Then by golly, off the couch you went with the red cape on your back, flying in the wind. Remember, I have two rambunctious little boys to attest to this truth. The faith you had was real, authentic, unwavering. You fell in love with the dream and employed faith to anchor it down. No wonder Jesus said in Mark 10:15, "Truly I tell you, anyone who doesn't receive the Kingdom of God like a little child will never enter it." He used childlike faith as the rubric to gauge who would make it into His Kingdom.

So I want you to go back to dreaming like a five-year-old. Yes, you read me correctly. Revisit what you did in the past. Interesting, that entertaining childhood dreams coupled with faith are actual clues leading to your God-given gifts. Begin to ask and answer the following questions: What did you want to be when you grew up? What gave you the most pleasure and joy? What made time pass by faster? What did you love to talk about? What put a smile on your face? What did you want to fix and make right? What constantly stayed on your mind? What would your parents say were your biggest likes and dislikes? Whom did you admire and why? Who was your childhood hero? Who saw something special in you at a young age, and what did they see?

These questions will wake up the snoozing dreamer in you. They will help find who was lost. Such inquiries are meant to reinvigorate and revive the dream that died in you. The constant questioning will serve as the AED machine shocking your heart so it can beat vigorously toward your passions. Take the time to examine yourself, and as Shakespeare would admonish, "To thine own self be true." Be honest with whom you feel inspired to become. Those persuasions are as real as the ground you walk on. Don't ignore them any longer. Live authentic to who you are—one bad-to-the-bone creation defined by immeasurable capabilities. This is you being true to the one person that matters most in your life—you. Also, remain aware and cognizant of affirmations given by people who desire your success. They could be pulling and pressing you into a higher level of living. Give them credit. They are aware of your higher standards for living more than you think.

My mother, Marilyn Trotter, tutored and grew my oratorical skills before I believed they ever existed. At four years of age, when Christmas and Easter rolled around at Little Welcome Baptist Church, Mom would hand me the longest speech she could find. While some of the other kids would recite their speeches emotionless, reading off paper with their heads down, never engaging the audience, Mom not only made me memorize my script; she also made me act as if I was the next Martin Luther King Jr. delivering freedom to his people.

Line by line, I would stand before her in practice to quote my speech verbatim with hand gestures to add life to my words, voice inflections to avoid sounding monotone. "Eyes up! Look at me, son." Mom would sternly say yet, at the same time, was somehow softly encouraging. I don't know how she pulled off this combo, but it worked. Marilyn, my speech coach, was breathing sparks into my gift, despite the lack of confidence and shyness I often exuded. Little did I know, these sparks would later turn into a massive wildfire.

I love this quote by Les Brown: "Sometimes, you have to believe in others' belief in you until your belief kicks in."

Mother nurtured my gift to life. She more than aided along a dream I didn't know was prevalent in the deep recesses of my heart. My hope is for you to have someone in your life who can see and affirm what makes you amazingly set apart. Mom's faith in me was the catalyst for what I do today: traveling the country inspiring masses to discover their God-given gifts en route to living in massive success. My motivation brand, NISANRPM, is making a dent in the world because at its core, the gift of encouragement was set ablaze.

Discovering your gift is easy. We, however, make it harder than necessary. Your gift has been with you from the very beginning. In fact, it was there before opening your brown, blue, green, or hazel eyes to the world. God expressed to the young prophet Jeremiah, "Before I formed you in the womb I knew you. Before you were born, I set you apart; I appointed you as a prophet to the nations" (Jeremiah 1:5). Like Jeremiah, your special powers, your call, your purpose existed before your first gulp of milk. It preceded your first cry, crawl, and cradle. God mapped out plans for Jeremiah prior to the prophet's existence. He specifically designed Jeremiah to speak to the nations. In Jeremiah 1:9, we see He even touched Jeremiah's mouth. He said, "I have put my words in your mouth." These profound yet simple words are one of my favorites. They are truly amazing. The Creator is so compelling, caring, and compassionate, and while appointing us, provisions are also made on our behalf to carry out our call successfully. He wants you to excel to the highest order. Like Jeremiah, you are set apart because of the gifts God installed in you. Like a computer programmer downloading sophisticated codes into a hard drive, you're hardwired with a gift. You've been touched by His grace too.

Today, at this very moment, boldly proclaim the fingerprints of God over your life. God's majestic power inexplicably simplifies the process of upgrading flawed, unequipped, mistake-ridden people like you and me. Yes. It's a common practice for Him to make something out of nothing, to take what is weak and make it strong, to plant greatness in the lives of the lowly and destitute. The acknowledgment of this miracle means you don't have to bother looking far for your gift; look within. You're a natural because of the handiwork of God. Like Jeremiah, He placed His hands on you.

Do you know what made Ken Griffey Jr. revered as a natural swinging the baseball bat? The Hall of Fame inductee and thirteen-time all-star had one of the prettiest strokes the game ever witnessed. I'm no baseball analyst, but research on his swat teaches us that the Kid, also known as the Natural, did less than most to hit home runs. Other competing MLBers were expending more effort into their swing than No. 24. Griffey did not overdo his motions at the plate. Seemingly each move, from top to bottom, gave him the power needed to hit the hardball over the fences. Ample power came from two places, the rotation of his hips and torso, as opposed to others who were frankly doing too much with their mechanics.

Take a deep breath. Be at ease, please. The point is to not overdo it. Relax. Your gifts come natural. Now let me forewarn you. It doesn't mean you will not have to work, nor does it mean life will forever be a bed of roses. There will be foul balls and even strike-outs, but the goal is to stack up home runs as you keep swinging. When you know you have the goods, it's more than half the battle. Be convinced—you have special ingredients naturally embedded in you from a supernatural source.

Fill in the Blanks

1. Entertaining childhood dreams coupled with faith are _____ leading to your God-given gifts.

2. Live authentic to who you are—one bad-to-the-bone creation defined by _____.

3. You're ____ with a gift! You've been ____ too!

Chapter Challenge

What did you want to be when you grew up? What gave you the most pleasure and joy? What made time pass by faster? What did you love to talk about? What put a smile on your face? What did you want to fix and make right? What constantly stayed on your mind? What would your parents say were your biggest likes and dislikes? Whom did you admire and why? Who was your childhood hero? Who saw something special in you at a young age, and what did they see?

Chapter 4

THE IRREVOCABLE GIFTS

Make generosity a part of your growth strategy.

—Anonymous

Behold generosity! Its opportunity is on every side of you and easy to notice when keeping an eye out. From the gentleman who generously gives his time to help a total stranger in need of jumper cables for a bad car battery to the mom baking cookies for her daughter's Little League softball team, giving is a powerful gift.

As a fitness entrepreneur, I am very fortunate to be surrounded by clients who love making contributions to our beloved community in the Susquehanna Valley of Central Pennsylvania. They are some of the most kindhearted, considerate, and unselfish people in my life. Members of my fitness tribe have literally given tons of food from their cupboards, donated several hundred pairs of shoes from their closets, stuffed gigantic trash bags full of clothes from their dressers, provided a slew of Christmas gifts for needy families in the area, and I have lost track of the amount of dollars clients graciously give away each year to several honorable local causes. I love TROTFIT Nation and our charitable work.

Generosity meets the multitude of physical and even emotional needs of those around you. We often hear recipients and beneficiaries rave about the gesture of giving, refusing to talk about the gift singularly. The emotional ramification of knowing you are loved and appreciated through the act of a total stranger giving his time and resources is immeasurable. Generosity keeps the world united through the everlasting, time-tested truth that we need one another to survive. One can consistently be generous no matter the number of commas in their bank account. Please note: you do not have to be rich to give. Many think of generosity in monetary terms. However, giving a smile to a passing stranger, complimenting your coworker on her new dress, offering words of encouragement to a friend who lost a loved one, or taking time to write a handwritten thank-you note to a mentor are some of the various ways generosity flashes its beautiful face.

Generosity reminds me of God's nature. Our Creator introduced generosity quite profoundly. He set the tone for how to give and give big by blessing you and me with earth. Psalms 115:16 says, "The heavens belong to the Lord, but he has given the earth to mankind." How wonderful to own the terrestrial sphere that houses the deep blue seas and whitecap mountains. You would be hard-pressed to find anything more incredible than our planet. God didn't choose to stop His giving there. He knew we needed gifts to have dominion over earth—to make it a place to leave our mark for His glory. So He chose to endow us with irrevocable gifts. "For God's gift and his call are irrevocable" (Romans 11:29).

The word *irrevocable* comes from the Greek word *ametameletos*, meaning "without regret," "not revocable," "no regret." So for starters, when God gives you a gift, it is permanently yours. He gave with pure intentions to ensure our gifts would be a blessing to us and an upgrade to the world. Your Heavenly Father, in part, made His name off being an absolutely awesome Gift Giver.

My wife, Yorelis, and I are in the process of teaching our three-year-old son, Onesimus, how to share. We get a kick out of asking Ony for a few of his last gummy bears held near and dear at the bottom of his purple candy cup. With a sparkle in our eyes and our pearly white teeth glistening, we put our palms out like paupers and beg, "Yum. May we have some gummies?" We then spectate the angst and wrestling taking place within the heart of our caramel-colored, curly-haired boy. With great hesitance, he reaches his hand into his cup and pinches out one selective gummy at a time (never the red one). The regret over his small act of kindness is so thick you can cut it with a knife. It is both funny and powerful to watch our son yield to the temptation of wanting it all for himself as opposed to giving a few little gummies to Mami and Daddy.

Oh, come on! Let's be honest. You can relate to Ony. You know how it feels to give begrudgingly. Whether it was giving the mighty dollar bill, lending an adored vehicle, or having to offer up undivided attention, you and I sometimes lack the state of eternal cheerfulness when it comes to our acts of charity. We know how it feels to give cheerfully versus the sting that accompanies giving with regret. God, however, only knows how to give in complete bliss. It satisfies His heart, makes it sing triumphantly, to give His possessions away. He knows you are going to make a positive impact on your family, friends, community, and haters with the gifts benevolently bestowed. When He gives you a gift, it is your gift for the world. Did you catch what I wrote? The major difference between God-given gifts and those given by people is this: people give gifts for you to keep, but God gives gifts for you to share with others.

With no regrets, He loves giving gifts to His children. He also enjoys witnessing your gifts on display, changing the lives of those around you. When I spread my love on Ony by kissing his juicy jaws, only to now see him returning the favor by wet-kissing Osias, his baby brother (who's absolutely adorable, I might add), my heart is warmed with joy. Do not reserve your gift any longer. Freely use it. Freely give it away. More details on how to share your gift will be discussed in a later chapter. Seeing a broader vision for your gift and the scope of its potential is more than adequate for now. Think less about you and more about the elevation of others locally, regionally, nationally, and globally—those who will change for the better because they have been exposed to your gift. Resist worrying about your cut when others have access to your gift. You will always be taken care of in the process of sharing what God freely gives you. A mentor taught me, "When you help people get what they want, they will help you get what you want." Trust me. It is far more fun when you allow others to experience the blessings attached to your gift. Behold generosity!

Fill in the Blanks

1. Make generosity a part of your _____.

2. For God's gifts and His call are _____.

3. Generosity keeps the world united through the everlasting, time-tested truth that we _____.

Chapter Challenge

Do one random act of generosity today. The more outrageous, the better!

Chapter 5

TALENT ADVISORY ALERT

> Your talent is God's gift to you. What you
> do with it is your gift back to God.
>
> —Leo Buscaglia

Are you afraid of your potential? Can you honestly answer this question? Have you even thought long and hard about the crazy possibilities of your audacious capabilities?

Read this famous quote by Marianne Williamson carefully:

> Our deepest fear is not that we are inadequate.
> Our deepest fear is that we are powerful beyond
> measure. It is our light, not our darkness, that
> most frightens us. We ask ourselves, who am I
> to be brilliant, gorgeous, talented, and fabulous. Actually, who are you not to be? You are a
> child of God. You're playing small does not serve
> the world. There is nothing enlightened about
> shrinking so that other people won't feel insecure
> around you. We are all meant to shine as children
> do. We are born to manifest the glory of God
> that is within us. It's not just in some of us, it's in
> everyone. And as we let our own light shine, we
> unconsciously give other people permission to do
> the same. As we are liberated from our own fear,
> our presence automatically liberates others.

Wow! If Marianne's words do not get you fired up, then check your pulse. She nailed it. Her heart-piercing words certainly convict and challenge me.

What are we afraid of? What can really stop us when we put our minds to it? Snap out of it, my dear reader. Do not be fearful of letting your light shine. We are powerful, strong, mighty, intelligent, disciplined, and courageous for the glory of God. Our lives have been crafted to be the evidence of these traits so much so when we walk down the street, people automatically know what we were born to do. Our gift should shine so bright it gives others the permission and freedom to carry out their own purpose on earth with boldness.

We hear you loud and clear, Marianne Williamson. Challenge accepted. No more playing in the Little League. It's time to go pro. Do you feel the rise in your heart prompting you to do more?

For the longest, I have been telling many of my friends and peers there is a book inside of them. The luxury of knowing their stories has inspired me to speak truth into their lives. In fact, one of my best friends, Brian C. Johnson, an author of seven books, invited me to his book signing for *The Room Downstairs*. He took my newly purchased hardback and wrote a few kind words, along with his autograph on the inside sleeve, after which he smiled big, looked me square in the eyes, and delivered these gut-wrenching words, "I'll be attending a book signing for you one day."

Shoot, Brian! Did you know I would be writing this very chapter the following day? Did you speak prophetically? Did God whisper those words into your ear?

I gently smiled, nodded and walked away from his table. I was inspired like a bat witnessing day turn to night...I was ready to fly.

When the idea of writing a book entered my mind, I felt inadequate about writing my thoughts on paper. Write a book? Really? "I'm too busy," "I have two kids," "I procrastinate too much," "I don't even have the pedigree." My mind needed to rest from the many ill-willed questions ruining my confidence. In my own point of view, writing a book simply was not possible, at least not at this stage of my life. I lived feeling more than inadequate about writing my thoughts on paper. Guess what changed the narrative for me? I began to believe God had already equipped me with special talents and abilities to write if I used my gift of encouragement.

Why not manifest the greatness He fearfully and wonderfully set in me since the foundations of the earth? No more dumbing down my unique skill set. Time-out for shortchanging my sphere of influence due to doubt and fear. I proclaimed: readers of *Born Gifted* will feel instant power because I decided not to play small.

Today, I declare a talent advisory alert. Get ready for torrential downpour. My faith is at supersized level. The more I write, the more He pours. My gift of encouragement is shining through this project, fueling every typed word.

Why was I letting those thoughts from before bully me around? Argh. I know better now. Now ring the alarm; my talent is on full blast. As I type this chapter, I believe God is bringing influential, renowned self-help and personal-development experts to write the foreword to *Born Gifted*. I do not have one ringing on my doorbell yet, but this is only chapter 5. Writing is my new mission. Finishing is my call. How can I be so confident and sure it will work out? Well, the answer lies in my bank account. You see, if you have enough faith in the bank, you can make a purchase on what you believe. I believe in the unthinkable, including writing my first book.

Hopefully, through my great escape of obstructive interrogation, you see the realm of possibilities that await you. You are talented. There is no question about it. What would be helpful is knowing the spiritual gifts God created for your advancement and the world's delight. Do you know them? Review the list I have provided below and see which sounds most like you. For some, you may quickly find your aha moment. Do not ignore it. For others, a spiritual gift test is necessary because you may have uncertainty or crossover among your gifts. Please note: you can be gifted in multiple areas, but usually one is more prevalent than the other. Enjoy navigating through the list, and have fun with this exercise. Set out on a goal to reintroduce yourself to you. Once you know exactly your God-given gift, the opportunity to be reinvented awaits in a brand-new way. Mark Twain said,

"The two most important days in our lives are when we are born and when we figure out why we were born." By going over this short list, you are well on your way to answering the why.

Here is the list and its accompanying scripture references:

- Exhortation, giving, leadership, mercy, prophecy, service, and teaching (Romans 12)
- Administration, apostleship, discernment, faith, healing, helping, knowledge, miracles, prophecy, teaching, tongues, tongue interpretation, wisdom (1 Corinthians 12)
- Apostleship, evangelism, pastorship, prophecy, teaching (Ephesians 4)
- Celibacy, hospitality, martyrdom, missionary, voluntary poverty (miscellaneous passages)

Let's spend some time reviewing some of my favorites. Warning: you may find that I am describing you in great detail. If so, don't ignore your thoughts. Focus on ways to grow in your gift. What you focus on the longest becomes the strongest. These gifts are very, very powerful. They are meant to advance and promote goodness throughout the world. Grab on to these words; you can be a real game changer with your gift.

Exhortation. I can go on and on about the gift of exhortation (encouragement) because God blessed me with it. Exhorters have the right words to say at the right time. We are uplifters and motivators. We can fire up wet wood. And there are several ways to encourage. Encouragers will send the inspiring Facebook inbox message to a friend going through a tough time. Our newsfeeds drip with positivity, inspirational quotes, and words of affirmation. Encouragers encourage themselves when needed. They search within for words of life. They also monitor their words to ensure more words of life are being spoken than words of discouragement. Encouragers are more likely to get random people divulging their stories to them and are told, "I know you don't really know me, but I feel compelled to share this with you."

Giving. The gift of giving is a special one. In a selfish "what's in it for me?" world, the gift of giving is vital to a well-functioning society. Givers don't give expecting something in return. The act of giving alone is enough to satisfy their soul. They give their time, energy, money, and resources. If a person needs help, their first thought is *What do I have to give to be of service?* Givers truly believe it is far better to give than to receive. They love witnessing the joy on the face of the receiver. Christmas, birthdays, and graduations are the givers' time to shine because their gifts are normally the most extravagant or well thought out. When givers are enjoying a bag of chips, they won't share one chip with you, they want you to eat the chips with them until the bag is empty.

Leadership. The gift of leadership is a forerunner. Leaders embrace the opportunity to be front and center corralling the troops. They make the tough decisions even if it spells making the unpopular call. They show up early and leave late. If a game-winning shot will bring home the championship, leaders want the ball in their hands. The gift of leadership is not for the faint of heart. Leaders have their emotional ups and downs because managing people is not easy. Leaders are worthy of a following because their shepherding is sincere for the people they serve. Leaders are dynamic and charismatic, and some are even envied and hated.

Mercy. The gift of mercy understands and lends a helping hand. It has sympathy and empathy. Those with this gift mourn over injustices. They hurt severely for those unfairly treated because they can relate to the deep wounds of being wronged. The merciful are incredibly patient and compassionate. They make routine hospital visits to the sick, spend time in nursing homes with the elderly, and pray for the forgotten and left out. They rejoice with those who rejoice and mourn with those who mourn. They are the shoulder when most needed.

Administration. The gift of administration directs traffic and keeps things organized. You find those who excel in this gift working as event coordinators, operation managers, secretaries, and personal assistants. Administrators are masterminds when it comes to scheduling and filling up planners. If someone is struggling with a chaotic agenda, an administrator is instrumental in helping devise a strategy. They will color code, number, and outline a step-by-step plan. My assistant is superb at keeping me on track: where I am and where I have to be next. She helps script my days. At the beginning of the week, we go over my schedule from setting sales meetings to my son's school drop-off and pick-up times. Administration is closely linked to the gift of leadership, but it's more aligned with task management and a dire focus on details.

Teaching. The gift of teaching breaks it down to common sense. Teachers don't teach to confuse. They teach to clarify. They love to see folks have the "aha" look on their face because of a thorough explanation. This gift enables them to make complex information as clear as spring water. Those with the gift of teaching are able to instruct in a variety of ways. They may use props to demonstrate their points, descriptive pictures for illustration, or any other fun way to make concepts and analogies stand out. Those with this gift have the range to appeal to various types of learners: auditory learners (people who learn best by sounds and words), visual learners (people who learn best by sight and pictures), and kinesthetic learners (people who learn best by touch and physical activity). Even in casual conversations, teachers make some of the best storytellers because they like hearing themselves talk and seeing the listener engaged in their words. Teachers share detailed sagas full of lessons and drama even with an audience of one.

Discernment. The gift of discernment is the itchy suspicion. It's foresight. It's the ability to see beyond what others cannot see. Discerners are able to sniff out a liar, fraud, or fake in a jam-packed room. Without hesitancy, they will say, "This person makes me feel creepy." They are smart and highly inquisitive. They are no easy sell and will not buy into the fluff. Those with the gift of discernment have strong feelings and use them to distinguish between who and what is right and wrong. People with strong discernment normally say things like "I feel," "I don't like," "The best way." Folks working with a discerning spirit cautiously ask for their thoughts because their feedback will be straightforward and sometimes hard to hear but truthful. The discerner is not trying to be rude; they simply keep it real. Discerners are problem solvers as they use their intuition and gut feeling to come to a decision. My wife has the gift of discernment, and I can tell you from personal experience, those with this gift absolutely love to hear when they are right. Feedback fuels their gift, and in turn, they bring thanksgiving to God. "Don't simply think it, boo. I want you to tell me," I hear my wife saying in my head, trying to take over my book!

Wisdom. The gift of wisdom is the ability to rightly use knowledge and intelligence. There are a lot of smart people who do dumb things. This is not wisdom. Wise people make good judgments. Those with this gift rely on their experiences to be a teacher. You do not have to be old and gray to have the gift of wisdom either. Wisdom enjoys listening to good counsel because they don't want to repeat the mistakes of others. The wise will pay close attention to errors and use what they have learned as a forewarning to help others. The gifts of wisdom and discernment are siblings, very close and nearly the same. People with wisdom read a lot; they are thirsty to apply favorable life concepts as upgrades.

The objective of covering the gifts above is to give you a taste of how cool your special powers can be. Spiritual gifts can steer you in what to do and who to become. The gifts' descriptors are like puzzle pieces ready to make the big picture a masterpiece. They help you make your contributions and play your role. Rather than aimlessly live, carry out your gift's potential and focus on what you do best.

If you need more help and counsel regarding your spiritual gift, visit my website NisanTrotter.com and enter your e-mail address to be a free, elite subscriber to my newsletter. Information discussing gifts, passions, talents, and dreams will come directly to your inbox and assist in your quest of self-discovery and self-mastery. You may also e-mail me at NisanRpm@NisanTrotter.com and ask me personal questions about your specific gift. I love hearing from the *Born Gifted* community.

Fill in the Blanks

1. Our deepest fear is that we are _____.

2. If you have enough _____ in the bank, you can _____ it.

3. Set out to _____ yourself to _____.

Chapter Challenge

Discover your spiritual gift.

Chapter 6

READ THE CONTEXT CLUES

> Without archives many stories of
> real people would be lost, and along with
> those stories, vital clues that allow us to
> reflect and interpret our lives today.

> —Sarah Sheridan

In order to lift people's spirit with words of life, you obviously have to talk. Do you agree? The right words need to fly off the tongue. This was an issue for me. Not only was I opposed to saying the right words; I didn't even want to talk. Let me explain why.

Unfortunately, either I sounded weird as a kid or classmates in middle school were really good at making me feel strange when I opened my mouth to talk. My voice was a bit raspy and soft. I have to admit, their impersonations sometimes sounded identical. Were they practicing at home before gathering with friends at school? Once the class bell sounded for break, kids huddled near the snack concession stand to take their jabs at me. Students ran wild on me like a prize horse out the gate for the Kentucky Derby. There was not a day that passed without being the center of jokes because of the way I spoke. Silence was my answer to avoid getting picked on and even bullied. It was terrible. I felt ostracized from society for the mere pitch and tone of my voice. I was mad, and sadness gripped me tight. The anger I had toward God for making me sound different from others nearly ruined me. Back then, my self-esteem was at an all-time low. A dark corner, so I could be left alone with my insecurities, looked attractive to me. Yup. I was not very fond of my middle school and early high school years. And this is exactly where the enemy wants you and me, stripped of our identity.

His joy is in our abandonment. He does not want anyone to recognize us. If we do not matter, especially to ourselves, he is pleased. Satan wants our power to be hidden and disguised from the world at large. With no voice, no words, he wants the final say. If you do decide to talk, then peers will take their turns ridiculing and mocking you. Even if you have something valuable to say, something worth sharing with the world, no one will truly hear the message because you sound weird at best and awful at worse. What a cunning device used by the enemy…to take away our sound. He knows that if we go silent and lose ourselves in the quiet, then we do not have a chance to positively impact the world with our gift. Satan would want nothing more than to cover up the truth about you and me. If he cannot completely get away with lies, then distorting the truth is his next best option. He wants to drown you out to insecure people who have their own battles, and he will use anyone or anything to make you shut up. The devil hates your voice; he wants you to feel the same way. He delights in foul play.

Remember Moses? He was God's ordained leader who set out to deliver the Israelites out of Pharaoh's hand. I love his powerful story prior to being a fearless, dynamic shepherd. Before taking charge of millions of stubborn people (i.e., Israelites), Moses presented his case before God as to why he was unfit for the assignment. In Exodus 6:30, Moses tells God, "I can't do it! I'm such a clumsy speaker. Why would Pharaoh listen to me?" Moses was trying to educate God on his speaking deficiency. How ludicrous.

Actually, God knew about the unskilled speech of Moses before deciding He would be His messenger. Never think your inabilities will disqualify you from what God wants to do in and through you. He is well aware of where you are and where He wants to take you. God's first priority was to show Moses who he could become despite the circumstances. His desire was to upgrade Moses's speaking ability and unveil the gift of leadership inside of him.

Can you imagine the frustration and ill-willed tactics of Satan while God was performing this awesome miracle in the life of Moses? While God was delivering Moses from his speech impediment, Satan was trying to keep him bound by fear. Perhaps Satan said, "Hey, who do you think you are talking to a king? You're a poor speaker. You have to be at least half crazy to believe Pharaoh will understand your words. You can't even say your ABCs without stuttering! Turn back and be silent!"

Ouch. You better believe the devil plays hardball when it comes to denouncing and distracting you from your purpose. He wants to hurt you right at the core.

My friend, let us no longer live in fear of our inadequacies and trust the incomprehensible work of God. The more we believe in the handiwork of God, the more powerful we become. God later tells Moses to "say everything I command you" (Exodus 7:2). And Moses obeyed. As a result, we never read of Moses's speaking problem again. What we do read, thereafter, is Moses frequently going to Pharaoh in confidence to proclaim what God is getting ready to do with perfect clarity of speech. I picture Satan fading in the background, furious at the fact Moses found boldness to speak up, even in the face of one mean and scary Pharaoh.

No longer embarrassed to speak among city streets, he is now letting the words fly off his tongue in loud altercations against Pharaoh, ruler of the most powerful empire known to man at the time.

The gifts of God have been given to declare warfare for those who believe in the saving grace of His son, Jesus Christ. It can stare down the meanest of foes. Carve this in your heart: Romans 10:11 says, "God will not allow you to be put to shame when you trust in him."

Trust what God has given you to win in life. His transferable power is not a fluke. It cannot be measured. Ignore the voices trying to talk down the potency of you and your gift. Resist the temptation to succumb to anything less than the value of you and your untapped potential when using your gift. Your destiny is the kingly palace.

Don't play along with the devil's games. He desperately begs for your partnership. He wants to detach you from the comforts your gift provides. You may assist him if you would like and live on the splintered patio of lies he has built. In Revelation 12:10, the Bible refers to him as "the accuser of the brethren." He will try to beat you up using false words. Picture his lies as a weak weapon, a water gun shooting among fiery missiles. Treat him like the old-school nursery rhyme claims, "Sticks and stones may break my bones, but words will never hurt me…nana nana, boo boo!" Combat his words at every whisper using the exact opposite. He calls you simpleminded, but you are complex and well thought out. He says you are a mess when you are actually well put together and a miracle like Moses. He claims you are nothing, but you are a whole lot of something with the "righteousness of God through faith in Jesus Christ" (Romans 3:22). He was trying to win at telling me I should not speak but lost that war a long time ago.

If you struggle to consistently speak words of empowerment, then I want you to pause from reading please. Go to my website right now, www.nisantrotter.com/borngifted, and click on Nisan's Dynamite Words Of Affirmation. Use this list everyday to build yourself up. You must affirm your greatness with words of truth and power. Don't allow your tongue to be your worst enemy any longer.

I need you to read the context clues. Thunder is a context clue for a rainstorm much like smoke is one for a fire. The place of your greatest pain, flaw, or failure is also the place where your gift has the chance to shine the most. Hurt is a context clue for your gift. My history would suggest I should not speak onstage in front of a crowd because I was the awkward-sounding kid in school, remember? Because my prepuberty voice inspired others to indulge in full-fledged mockery, paid motivational speaking gigs would seem like only a pipe dream and not a reality, right? However, in lieu of the discouragement that pained me, it also provided a gateway for the gift of encouragement.

Where pressures, pains, problems, wrongs, and hurts exist, be on the lookout for context clues as to where your gifting also resides. People who suffered from cruelty, meanness, unkindness, and a lack of compassion are the same ones now flourishing in the gift of mercy. They are able to minister in the place where their greatest pain existed. They know the pain of what it feels like to lack gentleness in their life, so their goal is to offer others something they did not receive. Why? Because they see the value of their gift firsthand and they are strongly compelled to fix what is wrong.

Those who endured terrible leadership ironically make great leaders. They have learned what not to do when positioned front and center. Perhaps in their past they lacked mentorship in their time of greatest need; today they understand misfortune and lend mercy. They empathize with the plight of the underserved. Fortunately, the gift of service rises in them as they eagerly lend their helping hands to impact and acknowledge social work.

If you are struggling to find your God-given gift, as difficult as it may be, revisit your history to see where pain derived. It may lead to tears and greater animosity toward those who did you dirty in the past. If so, pray and come up with a positive resolution to overcome those draining feelings. Recognize you are far better than who they said you were. Prove it by living a bright life—a life that shines before others. You are a beacon of success having not turned out the way they projected. Don't play or waddle in the mud of rumors, negativity or bad vibes folks tried to submerge you in. Get unstuck.

What context clues do you find when you go back to your past, never to stay there, but to learn and grow from? Was there any indications of a misunderstanding or misuse of your true powers because you simply did not know any better?

Perhaps you did not understand your value and worth, nor did you realize the uncountable accusations the enemies felt so obliged to force-feed you. Here is the beauty among the ashes I want you to be thankful for: You will surprisingly discover undeniable gifts as you endure struggle. You will be able to recover what was lost from the drama because a special handcrafted gift awaits. God is charitable and compassionate enough to exchange your pain for joy. He even provides context clues as to how you can make a world of difference in the lives of others by using traumatic experiences from your past that did not leave you for dead but left you with a transformative story.

Fill in the Blanks

1. This is exactly where the enemy wants you and me _____.

2. Never think your inabilities will _____ you from what God wants to do in and through you.

3. The place of your greatest pain, flaw, or failure is also the place where your gift has the chance to _____!

Chapter Challenge

Define the context clues leading to your gift.

Chapter 7

FRICTION

A gem cannot be polished without friction,
nor a man be perfected without trials.

—Lucius Annaeus Seneca

You are one of a kind. You cannot be duplicated or replicated. There is only one you. Nobody thinks exactly like you, nor do they act just like you. You see things differently and perhaps make fun shapes out of the clouds in the blue sky. You process situations unlike others, and you don't understand how others are so aloof of the facts. How could they be so bad at making a good decision? You simply see it the other way. Your skill set is personified by only one person—you. Perhaps you write like no other, sing magnificently, teach with astounding clarity, or easily provide hope to the hopeless. Maybe you are ridiculously witty and your insurmountable intellect makes itself readily available. Why is the algebraic equation extremely hard for everyone else but way too easy for you?

How about the capacity to lead stubborn people? Is this you? While many lose sleep and burn the candle on both ends, you, on the other hand, have poise and the unmitigated gall to have a decision made before punching the clock. You have a heart made of priceless gold. In it, you find room to love the folks several would consider the scum of the earth. You know where your gift resides. It sticks out like a red blinking traffic light at the end of a dark alley. Not only is your gift obvious; it carries a certain type of bravado. Family members and friends, even complete strangers, are impressed by it. When you are on, you flow with your gift in perfect harmony and balance. Oh, how fascinating to see people of all sorts sing your praises whenever they witness what only you can do.

There is at least one problem, however. It's not always peaches and cream regarding you and the workings of your gift. I don't want to be the bearer of bad news, but inevitably, in conjunction with your special powers is a resistance to them. Your gift carries friction like two scratch pads rubbing violently against each other. As my editor's mentor would say, "Your gift flipped around can be your biggest sin."

In fact, confirmation of your giftedness comes in the form of adversity and friction. Sometimes, the friction experienced is self-imposed too. Immaturity, laziness, lack of discipline, or even temptation to manipulate others thwarts the altruistic capabilities of your gift. Friction also surfaces as you cultivate your gift.

What if you are very good at giving but never put forth the time and attention to being great or, dare I say, elite? Have you been wise in dedicating a portion of life's precious minutes, hours, and days toward refining the God-given gifts inside of you? What if you are naturally good at administration but never read a personal-development book to learn how to grow and go to the next level with it?

Instead, you now see the friction between wasting time on vain pursuits and allocating time on what really matters—upgrading your gift. If only a redo were possible, then your focus would be on mastering your gift because of the type of return this process yields. In other words, you get more bang for your buck avoiding the idea fairy who whispers sweet nothings in your ear.

These types of voices are nothing short of a distraction meant to derail you from who you were created to be. They whisper sweet nothings like "Start XY&Z business, partner with the stranger-almost-friend on your neighborhood block, take out a big loan at EAD (Easy-to-Achieve Debt) Bank and start from scratch, and/or relocate to Hawaii. You will do so much better with warmer climate."

By simply focusing on your gift, the never-ending brainstorming of ideas serves as big-time friction to your limitless potential.

How much more potent would your gift be if you hired a mentor or coach? Do you know who is dominating the space you profess to be good in? Have you studied their efforts, took their courses, or watched their online videos? What if deep inside, you are jealous and envious of the super successful and you find the negative comments about them in the tabloids highly entertaining? Yet the friction of working to be their equal or at least coexist with them on the same playing field turns your stomach into knots.

What if you began to admire them instead and learn from their expertise?

Putting in real work toward making your gift better is the downfall of many people because they lose hope, get tired of the rat race, don't have enough patience, climb the corporate ladder unethically, and despise those at the top of it. Don't allow this to be your story. Proverbs 14:30 says, "Envy rots the bones." The hate war among the marketplace, in the church, and even amid family members and friends can physically bring hardship to your body. It will also take a toll on your mind. So how do you bring substance and meaning to it all when this type of friction is running rampant in today's world or closer to home and currently alive in your life?

Well, for starters, surround yourself with the winners of the game. Build strategic partnerships. Surround yourself with overcomers. Stand next to those who are the best at your gift—those who can write the manual. Many of the greats have paid the cost, bought the t-shirt, and now they are wearing it (with no wrinkles). You would be surprised at how generously they would share their intellectual capital if the right person came along with the right questions. And that, my dear reader, is you. Time-out for trying to reinvent the wheel or even attempting to do it on your own. Make friends with the A-listers. Take them out to lunch. Send them an e-mail. Offer dinner in exchange for some advice. Sometimes, in order to be a winner, you have to hang around someone with a polished diamond ring in their credenza, which represents the spoils of victory. Position yourself among life givers, folks who will speak positive words of affirmation about you and your gift. The enemy does not want you around people who will upgrade your potential. Instead, he would rather have you aimlessly flap your wings like a chicken for a few cheap thrills of airtime, as opposed to soaring in the highest of clouds with the eagles. He wants to see you crying at night, defeated on every end.

You must have a winning mentality even if life isn't matching up to your thought life.

Your bank account has more commas and zeros in your mind, but in reality, it appears as if it's headed for the red. You are fascinated by the ins and outs of becoming a serial entrepreneur, but your current nine-to-five job wreaks boredom.

Beloved, the breakthrough you are destined to have at this stage in life is going to come by way of learning from the winners. Who is the veteran in your corner, circle, city, or country who has been there and done that? Find the person who will encourage you and say, "If I can do it, so can you! You're an overcomer too. You are more than a conqueror!" Those words of affirmation will be like gasoline to your fire.

I want you around someone who is legitimately a thoroughbred at their craft. The person who actually knows what they are talking about is the one in whom you should have a vested interest. One of my greatest pet peeves is listening to someone who does not know what they claim to know. I would rather receive counsel from a person who has been through the fire and learned their lesson than harken to an individual who speaks only in theory. You need somebody who has the gift of wisdom and encouragement, someone bold enough to say "The boyfriend or girlfriend you are dating is not your type," "Look elsewhere. This job dumbs down your skill set," "Put an application in elsewhere. This apartment does not match the goals and vision you have for yourself," "Save more money for an upgrade." Want to make a giant step toward wisdom? Get the right person to help reset your GPS and overcome friction.

The next principle on how to overcome friction that accompanies your gift is setting your focus on keeping the main thing, the main thing. Disarm yourself from what I call WMD (weapons of mass distractions). Rid your cargo of unnecessary items. Do you really need help identifying what they are? I am sure some of your plaguing distractions immediately came to mind. It is the hours and hours of television watching, surfing the worldwide web to do frivolous shopping or news binging, constantly making status updates on social media or eyeballing others, endlessly flipping through the plethora of magazine subscriptions, and the list goes on and on. Come up with healthy stopping points.

I had a bad habit of watching highly entertaining sports talk shows. My eyes glued to the tube whenever the polarizing sports anchors aired. My wife paid notice to the passing hours, watching the same shows over and over again. She realized my lack of productivity in every fleeting highlight. It was unbecoming of me to continue this pattern, and we both knew it. If the popular sports shows had forever captured my attention, which undoubtedly was their goal, then I could have kissed *Born Gifted* goodbye. If I had steered away from keeping the main thing, the main thing, my gift of encouragement through writing would have been sacrificed.

You see, there is a risk taken with every attractive distraction made of fool's gold. The real treasure is found within your gift and God's given assignments. Keep the twenty-four karats as the focus and eliminate distractions by dialing in on what makes you, you. Please understand you were designed for more than being tossed to and fro with every passing distraction. James 1:8 cries out, "A double-minded man is unstable in all his ways." To be double-minded means to be pulled in multiple directions at one time. This is not a recipe for being effective. Distractions present unstableness. Have you ever been irritated by a text-message chime or notification ding that breaks the rhythm of your focus? It takes you at least ten minutes to get back on track. Very frustrating, right?

In order to break the pattern of distractions, you have to put your foot in the ground, draw a line in the sand, and say no to temptations begging for you to veer off course. Tell yourself no often and establish boundaries. Doing this alone will make you feel more important because you are creating necessary structure. Guidelines for your day will create the life you want. Script times for work, play, and leisure. You are too gifted to live by an unstable plan. The purposes and vision for your life thrive off routine, not chaos. Set alarms on the smartphone that awaken your senses saying "Enough is enough" whenever you subconsciously drift into too much TV, Internet, or any other mindless indulgence. Your gift shall not die in the hands of distractions. Engage in an all-out, intense level of concentration for an extended period of time when it comes to doing what you were created to do on earth. Now that is a recipe for greatness!

If you struggle with weapons of mass distraction and desire more structure in your life, particularly in the mornings, then head on over to www.nisantrotter.com/borngifted. Here, I share my awesome morning routine. It's a detailed script designed to help me dominate my days as soon as I rise out of bed. You'll gather some great ideas for your own productive day.

Finally, the most challenging level of friction you will face regarding your gift is striking out with it. Yes, you are going to strike out, you are going to strike out, you are going to strike out. I had to provide the news flash at least three times so you can remember who shared this first. Striking out is not bad; it is necessary. The wound of swinging and missing with your gift may hurt initially, but if you stick with the process, a home run is expected in the game plan. I wish being the absolute best at the outset were true; it rarely, if ever, works that way for anyone. The journey of growth will be cumbersome, to put it politely. But those who have the fortitude to ride out the high and low tides, enjoy the coveted stardom and success that eventually comes with the territory called perseverance. Did you read that correctly? Eventually.

Baseball teaches that one can be great and still strike out. Major-league baseball players of yesterday and today are not even close to batting .500 from the plate. This means hitting the ball and getting on base at least 50 percent of the time is highly unlikely of any pro. Oh, and you can forget about the average Joe swinging the pine at this success rate.

Records show the best batting average in the MLB history was roughly .400. That is 40 percent being the top of the pecking order and an all-time record. Let's run a bit further using this example. The good news is, you don't have to knock it out of the park. You don't have to hit doubles or triples. You don't even have to hit to get on base 60 percent of the time, which is D average by school-grading metrics. Your objective should be reduced to swinging to get on base. Overcome the inertia of getting started, gain momentum, and swing, batter, swing!

It is far better to carry the mentality that you don't have to be perfect to be gifted, versus feeling like you always have to get it right. You can fall down with your gift only to get back up again. You can take a swing and miss, only to get back in the batter's box. Keep working on your swing; do not dare give up. Make the adjustments in route to greatness. Zig Ziglar said, "You don't have to be great to start, but you have to start to be great." Pressure is not the only thing that produces diamonds. Stubborn perseverance, despite friction, has a big role in developing you into a gem.

Fill in the Blanks

1. Confirmation of your giftedness comes in the form of _____ and _____.

2. Get around people who are _____.

3. Your gift shall not die to _____.

4. It is far better to carry the mentality that you don't have to be _____ to be gifted, versus feeling like you _____ have to get it right.

Chapter Challenge

Which one of the three types of friction is most prevalent in your life?

- Not having a mentor/encourager
- Weapons of mass distraction
- Striking out

What advice, specifically from this chapter, will you embrace today to overcome friction?

Chapter 8

MAC-AND-CHEESE GREATNESS

There's still time for greatness.

—Andrew Craig

It was Thanksgiving 2015, and I phoned my beautiful, milk-chocolate-skinned, Southern belle mother to discuss the macaroni-and-cheese dish I made for the first time. Quite proud of my concoction, I began to ramble, looking through the frosted windows of my cozy little home in Lewisburg, Pennsylvania. "After pouring in the condensed milk slowly, put the second layer of sharp-shredded cheddar cheese on top. Make sure you get the name-brand stuff, Ma. Once you place it in the oven, wait to make sure the top is golden brown, then—" Mom kindly stopped me midsentence and, as humbly as she could, in her Alabama accent, said, "Son, you can spare me the details. I know how to make mac and cheese. I can make it four and five different ways. You will be great when you learn how to make mac and cheese good without the cheese."

"Wow! Wait, what? How do you make mac and cheese good without the main ingredient?"

She didn't mean to steal my thunder; nevertheless, she did. I knew she was very proud of me, and I'm sure her words came from a good place. What she did not realize, however, is the deeper lesson embedded in her words. My heart was pounding from the impact of the subliminal teaching she resonated.

Mom has cooked most of her entire life. My grandmother birthed ten kids (five boys and five girls), and Mom was the older of the bunch, which meant she bore the responsibility of combing her sisters' hair for school, refereeing her brothers' wrestling matches, and cooking for the whole gang. Her love and history of cooking parlayed over to kitchen prepping for a number of popular chain restaurants in town. I remember her coming home smelling like fresh bell peppers, shrimp skewers, salted mushrooms, and every other food you would like to devour. Mom would set up all the essentials and premade foods for the entrées at the restaurants, especially their signature dishes.

She eventually moved on to head cook for a well-established retirement home. She loved this job because it dealt with her passion. When Mom was in the back kitchen working her magic, the elderly residents would salivate at the mouth over breakfast, lunch, and dinner. Whispers would roam around the cafeteria tables as they feasted: "This is so good!" "Marilyn really knows what she's doing back there." Plus, it's also fair to mention, my mom cooked for her three collegiate scholarship athletes. Obie, Shelby, and I had gigantic appetites, especially after our evening ball practices. We absolutely loved coming home to Mom's spices and blends permeating in the air; it smelled so good you wanted to eat the entire house! Mom is a natural. She will use measuring tools from time to time, but a pinch of this and pinch of that, along with her eye and taste test, is her preferred method of cooking. She possesses the know-how when it comes to making tons of recipes from scratch, pretty much eliminating the need for a cookbook in her kitchen.

"It's all in the head. If I tell you, I'll have to cut you," she says with a smirk to those asking for too many details regarding her delicious masterpieces. When you do the math, Mom has been cooking for more than thirty-five years. So who was I to try to teach her on Thanksgiving Day? Without any uncertainty, it should have been the other way around. Her mac-and-cheese dishes are top-shelf, and of course, I am a wee bit biased, but it's the truth, I promise. The inherent message in her, "Son, you can spare me the details" is very simple to understand: Greatness takes time!

To download Marilyn's Magnificent Mac-and-Cheese visit www.nisantrotter.com/borngifted. A mac-and-cheese photo will be available. Click there to get mom's delicious recipe. I talked her into giving up some top secret information. Don't take it for granted - ha!

Time is the secret ingredient for greatness. It certainly does not happen overnight. You do not pull up to greatness drive-through and order a PhD with a side of MBA then speed off with your hand outside the car window to grab your purchase. Greatness is not like fast food. You cannot nuke it in a microwave. You have to put it in a slow cooker. Greatness has to marinate overtime. Remember this: if there were a fast track to greatness, then everyone would have been riding it.

The fast-paced society we live in screams louder and louder for everything to be available on demand. The Internet pop-up solicitations require immediate attention, text messages buzz your phone begging for a quick shorthand response, microwaves nuke food so it can be hot and steamy on the spot. They all scream, "Give it to me now!" And they are conditioning us to want greatness faster than ever before. If greatness were a tree, then its roots would be a consistent effort toward your goals, the branches would be unwavering patience to see them through, and its leaves would be Father Time ticking toward your maturity.

I know you feel specialness inside of you. Your gifts and passions are brewing and bubbling. You should be a recognizable figure to whom folks pay homage. Like the popular sitcom *Cheers* that aired in the early eighties to nineties would suggest, "Everybody should know your name and be glad you came." The major contributions you are destined to make in the world are nothing short of greatness. However, in order to play on the stage of greatness, you not only have to pay your dues and know your stuff; you also have to be willing to let time take its course. I am fully aware instant-made influencers exist in today's marketplace. I have witnessed the guy or gal who, out of nowhere, is now a reality TV star. However, most of those who are revered and respected on a world-class level will tell you their success took time. They were at one point a no-name. The type of gift cultivating within you has substance and cannot be downgraded to the way sensationalists make it appear. Celebrate those who arrive early because hatred does not help.

Now let's focus on you. You will be thorough in every sense of the word upon arrival. Prepackaged with the goods to make a significant impact on others, you will be time-tested, able to withstand the volatile storms of raging winds trying to blow out your gift. You will not vanish or fall down under pressure; God is building your greatness, and He is not doing it halfheartedly. It takes a lifetime to become an overnight success, so please be patient with your greatness. Do not get frustrated when you see less talented people shine. Do not throw a pity party because a global broadcast is not being made about your gift. Do not lose your cool because your limelight is dimly lit and no one can see you, for now. This will change. It is simply not your time, yet. Be patient. James 5:7 says, "Be patient, then, brothers and sisters, until the Lord's coming. See how the farmer waits for the land to yield its valuable crop, patiently waiting for the autumn and spring rains."

We can learn a lot from the farmer in this passage. The farmer is a prime example of patience. Of course, even though the farmer has a hand in producing the crops, the crops actually produce his livelihood. Without fruits and vegetables in his field, how can he survive? He will not eat, and he will not get paid for his toil. However, he is not identified by uncanny nervousness, irrational thoughts, or extreme agitation but, rather, resolute patience. He takes care of the no. 1 priority: planting seeds. He places the rest of the duties in the Master's hands. The farmer knows he does not have the power to make crops. He knows he cannot change the seasons. It is simply outside of his capabilities to make the blue skies rain. So what does he do? He waits patiently. Not only does he wait patiently; he waits patiently on what he cannot control. There is also an implied trust in his demeanor because he knows the Lord has saved the day (better than Superman) with harvest from earlier years. As a result of these stones of remembrance, he is conditioned to perpetually trust and wait on God to change the seasons, make it rain, and bring forth vegetation. So how does this apply to you?

I want you to be patient with your gift. Do not expect to be a rock star overnight. Could you be exceptional at the very beginning? Absolutely. Go ahead and prepare for your success by peppering time on top of your gift, the way my mom would pepper my favorite shepherd's pie dish. Embrace the farmerlike characteristics described above, and control what you can control. Plant seeds of greatness in your life by putting in the work, but first, make sure to till your landscape as precedence for a bountiful harvest.

Tilling is the preparation needed for farming to make the conditions right for growth. Tilling is necessary to turn dry, crusted ground into fertile soil. How can this be applied to you?

Your gift will not flourish in the wrong environment. Make sure that what you are listening to, watching, and entertaining yourself with is good soil that will continually unfold the greatness of your gift. Why? Because your eyes and ears are the gateway to your heart, and you need a good heart to win, not a contaminated one flooded with the senseless dramas of the world. Tilling prevents weed growth. When you put in the right amount of preparation to be great at your gift, the weeds designed to suck the life out of you have no place to breathe. Your time used to prepare and mature what you do best safeguards against weeds. Weeds of fear, anxiety, negativity, and jealousy die under the power of your intentionality and focus.

When seeds are planted in a good environment, your job suddenly becomes a patient wait. Have a good attitude here. Joyce Meyer says, "Patience is not the ability to wait, but the ability to keep a good attitude while waiting." In short, be like the farmer, trust the Lord, wait patiently, and let good old-fashioned time seep into the pores of your gift. Soon, you'll have mac-and-cheese greatness within you.

Fill in the Blanks

1. _____ is the secret ingredient of greatness.

2. Control what you can _____.

3. Weeds of _____, weeds of _____, weeds of _____, weeds of
    _____ die under the power of _____.

Chapter Challenge

What are you trying to rush? Take a moment and write down the items in your life being rushed versus applying more patience and time.

Chapter 9

CHARACTER > GIFT

> Be more concerned about your character
> than your reputation because your character
> is who you really are, while your reputation
> is merely what others think you are.

> —John Wooden

The pursuit of greatness does not trump building virtuous character. Upstanding character will forever be more important than the potency of your gift. On the surface, it may appear as if your gift is inspiring a revolution, but your character is the key driver pushing the needle forward. A person's character can easily go undetected too. Perhaps some would argue it is nearly impossible to walk down the busy streets of New York City and select folks who have good character. I'm obliged to agree. Praiseworthy character consist of intangible, honest, and ethical traits. Someone's character is their emotional intelligence. So two good willed people can be good in different ways because character is defined by the individual. One person's superb character may lead to serving chicken noodle soup at the homeless shelter downtown, whereas another may be driven to work extremely hard as a blue-collar making an honest living to support the wife and kids. Both examples show the significance morals play in spurring on commendable actions. This begs the question, what is at the core of who you are?

I know the focus has been on your gifts, but please understand, admirable character should pilot the evolution of your gift and what you plan to do with it. Don't tell me how gifted you are at writing, singing, dancing, teaching, preaching, leading, painting, or speaking yet you take advantage of those in awe of your talent and God-given abilities. Beware of the temptation to cunningly lord your power over people for selfish gain. "I would never do that, Nisan." I can hear you now. I am not saying you would intentionally hoodwink anyone. However, if you do not keep your guard up by keeping underlying motives pure, then selfish and wicked schemes can creep into your heart before noticing their occupancy. It can happen to the best of us.

King David, one of God's chosen mighty men, who was much anointed, expressed in Psalms 139:23, "Search me, O God, and know my heart! Try me and know my thoughts." If the king of that time had to pray such a prayer, then what about you and me? His effort has a number of implications. First off, there is a fundamental difference between *search* and *look*. David did not say "Look at me"; he said "Search me." David humbly solicits God to search him with the hopes of the Maker finding something wrong, something unfit, something that should not be present. Lacking pride yet demonstrating boldness, David asked God to do a hard thing—not hard for God, but hard for him. Had David asked God to merely look at him, then one can conclude he only wanted God to view him in appreciation or admiration. Instead, he went deeper and asked the King of kings to search him like a professional cleaning service vacuuming dust out of an Arizona desert home.

Not everyone wants to be searched. To search means one will carefully and thoroughly look to discover or find. David anticipates God will find impurities in his heart. He knows if his heart is off-kilter, his gift will not be hooked on doing what is right in the sight of God.

God's searching is also a private matter. David is asking the Creator to intimately oversee an investigation of his heart, something the sovereignty of God can only perform. I am glad he asked God to clean house and not man. Man cannot handle the junk in your closet, nor should they be exposed to it either. Because folks view you as a king or queen, it is tough for them to comprehend how someone so gifted can have a litany of flaws. Watch out for this trap. The fans who revere, respect, and acknowledge your renowned gifts may be the source of what makes you want to hide your mess from God. Please do not avoid the heart check by God. Although it may be quite flattering to be appreciated by the masses (because of your superpowers), do not make the mistake of foregoing the opportunity to get in the face of God or, better yet, allow Him to get in your heart. He needs to frisk your heart, and He's well qualified to do so. Far be it from you to reach the highest of highs only to be made low because of the foul temptations and icky nasties interwoven in your heart.

Today, shocking news and scandalous tabloids are no longer shocking and scandalous. The world is now desensitized to church leaders, business experts, and government officials who miss the mark of integrity and now have to face the dark music of their corruption. Some allow the pursuit of riches, cares of this world, or the desire to please others to be a setup for failure. Man-made pedestals are dangerous and can be an enemy to God's future plans for you. People praise your success, and then pride swells in your heart. Before long, you are puffed up, and this *edges God out* (the acronym for EGO). "He resists the proud and gives grace to the humble" (James 4:6). Remember this: You want to be on the grace-receiving end and not the alternative. God wants to embrace and receive you rather than resist, but pride puts off a foul smell to His nostrils. He can't help but push away because it stinks. Beware. Humbly go before God in devotion for a search because He would love the chance to clean out the hurt, deceit, fear, anxiety, hate, and selfishness present in your heart. You may not even know it's there, but He does; He's an expert cleaner.

David knew this full well. I imagine David thinking, "Sure, I'm a king, but that doesn't make me the King. I must return to an intimate, devoted life with God so He can unveil and show me, me and, best of all, fix me." God knows you better than you know yourself, and He has the power to uncover blemishes that threaten the potential of your gift. Allowing Him to refine your character also gives assurance that He can trust you to handle your gift appropriately. He doesn't want you to hurt others due to the misuse of your gift and its purpose. He is not only in the gift-giving business; He is also in the character-building business.

So beyond the proper application of your gift, you may be asking, "What else does God search for in my character?" Well, God also looks for what He produced in you since the beginning of your walk with Christ: fruit!

Galatians 5:22 talks about the fruits of the spirit being "love, joy, peace, patience, kindness, goodness, faithfulness, gentleness, and self-control." It may be hard to believe you have been gifted these qualities by the Savior, but trust the "fearfully and wonderfully" made work of God in your life. In order to be productive with your gift, it is imperative to have the fruits of the spirit. Your character should be made up of these virtues because they drive your gift forward.

Do you want to be a peaceable lawyer in the courthouse when tension rises? Do you want to be a highly successful entrepreneur who has remarkable self-control? Do you want to be a patient event coordinator pointing out directions for teammates who follow your command? Do you want to be the school counselor full of joy when students look for guidance and help? It makes a huge statement to others when they know there is something bigger, more powerful than you governing your efforts.

I cannot be a successful leader of my family without the fruits of the spirit. Being a leader is a gift God has generously given me. One of the ways I grow in this gift is by learning how to be more patient, kind, and loving when leading. I know my family truly appreciates my maturity in this area. My wife and kids are not in love with my gift; they are in love with me. To them, I am hubby and daddy, not Nisan, the Fitness Preacher. Should I ever lose this perspective (which I will not), then I lose them.

The no. 1 place I want to be seen as a superstar is in my household. I want to win in other places too—on the job, at work, and in the church. However, I never want Yorelis, Onesimus, and Osias to resent that I'm a fitness entrepreneur, minister, author, and motivational speaker to the world at large yet, when I get home from work, I'm negative and short-tempered and the remote-clicker zombie dad showing less than a single ounce of leadership and love toward them. Love begins in the home.

Home is the place where you are not obligated to turn on, so use the environment to introspectively look at how you lead those inside of it. Home reveals your true nature because you don't have to impress anyone. Could your kids be impatient, unforgiving, and mean because they see those actions in your leadership as a parent? Ouch. Begin to improve your character at home, and make it a priority. You will find it difficult at times, of course. Sometimes, we are most caring and thoughtful to those outside our household. However, when we think more highly of our home and those who dwell in it, our growth as a leader can evolve to the next level. Home provides a stage to see who you really are versus what others think you are. Ask your family members "How am I doing as a father/husband/mother/wife/brother/sister/daughter/son? What areas can I improve?" You may have to slow them down from the amount of feedback they throw your way; trust me from personal experience. However, let their words resonate.

At the helm of every gift, underlying it all, you should find the fruit of your character and the fruits of the spirit (love, joy, peace, patience, kindness, goodness, faithfulness, gentleness, and self-control). And if you're strong in one fruit but fall short in another, it's okay. You are not perfect, but by the grace of God, you are perfecting. So be brutally honest with yourself. It can only help.

Men and women may be impressed by the bright lights of your shining gift, but God is more fascinated with you as His child. He wants to see improvements with how you treat your administrative assistant; show more love to him or her. He wants to admire the patience you show the checkout clerk at the grocery store who rings your order wrong; smile and don't be disgruntled. He wants you not to lose your cool but instead to operate in peace when someone calls you a nasty name. The great Billy Graham said it best, "When money is lost, nothing is lost. When health is lost, something is lost. When character is lost, all is lost." Keep your character intact. You have too much to gain with it.

Fill in the Blanks

1. On the surface, it may appear as if your gift is inspiring a revolution, but your _____ is the key driver pushing the needle forward.

2. Humbly go before God in devotion for a _____ because he would love the chance to clean out the hurt, deceit, fear, anxiety, hate, and selfishness existent in your heart.

3. Men and women may be impressed by the bright lights of your shining gift, but God is more fascinated _____.

Chapter Challenge

At the beginning of your "quiet time," ask God to search your heart and reveal what's inside. Then pray for Him to clean out what He doesn't want there and to replace it with nothing but goodness.

Chapter 10

I QUIT

> Letting go has nothing to do with "quitting."
> Ask yourself, "Am I sticking it out, or am I
> staying stuck." You know yourself best.
>
> —Alex Elle

Your gift will make you quit. Did I sink your boat? Did I rock your world? Did I at least make you think twice? You have heard the words "Keep going," "Keep fighting," "Ride it out till the end." Heck, even the great Winston Churchill is famous for saying "Never give up. Never give up. Never give up!" Apparently, his statements were so profound it was necessary to say them three times to drive home the point.

"Do not stop playing on the Little League baseball team" or "Finish the varsity cheerleading season" is the advice you remember hearing as a youngster. Throughout your life, you have been conditioned to value the merit of sticking it out, rolling with the punches, and by any means whatsoever, doing everything within your power to never quit. Quitting makes you a loser. Quitting means you lack focus. Quitting means you are weaker, lesser, and unable to do what big boys and big girls do—stay on board for the long haul. So never jump ship and always surf the waves of perseverance and eventually you will be in a better place than where you began, right? Wrong.

What if I completely flipped the script to suggest quitting is what your gift will force you to do? "But wait, Nisan. Aren't you the guy who just told me greatness takes a lifetime? Didn't you insinuate constant focus is pivotal for success?" The answer is yes. Yes, I did. And, I don't back off from those claims one bit. However, I see far too many people with too much potential settling for life's second, third, and fourth best. They are not sensitive to time's valuable stake in their life. So unfortunately, they continue in the heartbreaking, degrading relationship too long. They go through the motions at the underpaying job too long. They eat greasy, sugary foods too long. To them, I say, quit while you're ahead! In fact, there is a boatload of profit to be made in quitting. Ecclesiastes 3:1–8 says,

> There is a time for everything, and a season for every activity under the heavens: a time to be born and a time to die, a time to plant and a time to uproot, a time to kill and a time to heal, a time to tear down and a time to build, a time to weep and a time to laugh, a time to mourn and a time to dance, a time to scatter stones and a time to gather them, a time to embrace and a time to refrain from embracing, a time to search and a time to quit searching, a time to keep and a time to throw away, a time to tear and a time to mend, a time to be silent and a time to speak, a time to love and a time to hate, a time for war and a time for peace.

Did you notice that everything has a time?

Now for starters, if there is a time for everything, then quitting is part of the equation. When you read the passage carefully, quitting is sprinkled throughout the text. "A time to tear down, a time to quit searching, a time to throw away" are fancy ways of quitting or starting over at best. The key word is time, of course. Understanding and discerning the right time is significant and must be acknowledged. Sometimes, you have to notice when time has expired and the opportunity to quit is made available. You are reading me correctly. Quitting is opportunistic. Seek it out.

On February 29, 2012, Leap Day, I turned in my two-week resignation as annual fund manager at Bucknell University. It was a surreal experience. I quit. I quit a nice-paying career with upward mobility and benefits. I quit the chance to travel major northeast cities like Baltimore, Philadelphia, and New York and break up the monotony of living in a small town with little to do. I quit working with a substantial budget that afforded me nice hotel stays and fancy meals. I quit meeting one-on-one with successful, talented young alumni, listening to their colorful work-life and play-life stories as I solicited monetary support for an institution we both loved.

I was not an underperforming fund-raiser. In fact, I was doing quite well with my responsibilities of meeting my two basic yet big quotas: visiting lots of alumni and raising lots of mula for the university.

However, while at Bucknell, there was another passion brewing in me to become a fitness entrepreneur, specifically a fitness boot camp owner. I've wanted to have my own business as far back as I can remember. I was ready to trade in my shirt and tie for Dri-FIT clothing and a pair of sporty sneakers. My endeavors as a part-time "fitprenuer," so it's called, started very small and meager. I didn't own or rent a building. Nope. The downtown public park in the early mornings, before going into the office, was where the adventure began. The sometimes cold and rainy weather, wet and slippery grass, and bloodsucking mosquitoes also came with the territory. Initially, tons of clients did not come flocking in droves to get in shape. Two clients to start was more like it, and little by little, transformation after transformation, scores of fun-loving people started calling TROTFITNESS Fit Body Boot Camp their fitness home. My wife and I started to realize my part-time boot camp paycheck was equivalent to my full-time paycheck received from Bucknell.

Then, one day, while working at my desktop computer at Bucknell, I felt a very strong nudge in my heart. It was a whisper from God: "Why are you still here?" It scared the living daylights out of me. Quickly, I ran down the three flights of stairs in my office building. I then scampered into the bathroom to douse my face with water, looked myself intensely in the mirror, and asked, "Did I really feel that? Did I really hear that? 'Why are you still here?'" I was nervous. My heart was racing. Yet I felt empowered to be fearless. This experience was exactly what I needed to jump full-time into my dreams of being a business owner. Before making a bold move, I called my wife on the office phone. She worked across campus in admissions. "Babe." I paused. "I believe it's time." She knew exactly what I was talking about. Yorelis has always been my greatest support. "Do it, Babe. God's got us," she reassured.

So on Leap Day, I took a leap of faith into my destiny. I quit. This date will live in infamy. Quitting flung open the door so my gift of encouragement could strut through. Imagine me holding on to the comforts of my old job. I had a great time there. There are no regrets from the experience garnered, but imagine the agony that would have been burning inside me had I not been brave enough to quit. Delving into the arena of health and fitness has led to having a profound impact on thousands of people in my local community and beyond.

Clients have shown the utmost appreciation for shedding unwanted pounds and inches from their bellies, thighs, arms, and so on. Many have expressed gratitude for either needing to shop for a brand-new wardrobe or being able to fit back into old clothes that once were supertight. The fact clients' husbands (or wives) are now paying attention to them, again, and showering them with compliments is a big testimonial that comes regularly. I should not solely talk about aesthetics because members of TROTFIT nation also brag about getting off the pills, potions, or medications for their ailments. They love boasting about lower blood pressure or lower cholesterol as a result of working out in boot camp. Their doctors are surprised by the jaw-dropping results earned within a span of six months to a year, and sometimes even shorter. I absolutely love it when a client raves about being able to play with their energetic kids without getting winded or having the confidence and self-esteem to try something really challenging like those crazy 5K obstacle course runs that are advertised. Evidence of the physical, mental, and emotional changes among my sphere of influence seemingly never cease. If I were to continue with the transformations that have occurred over the course of five-plus years, then the "I Quit" chapter would be known as the never-ending one.

However, I figured you would enjoy a few real-life testimonials from outstanding clients who have earned no-less-than-stellar results in our fitness community. So don't simply take it from me. Here's the proof:

> I've never been more motivated to workout. There's something about TROT that makes you want to reach higher and push harder. You can't call it a gym because it's in a different league. It's been a lifestyle change for me. I have more energy and can easily maintain my new weight. And, I'm proud of the new and improved me.
>
> —Lucille

> I decided to sign up for TROTFITNESS in hopes that I would drop a few pounds. I tried various other classes, programs, videos, and even running. None of them seemed to keep my interest like TROT. After walking into my first session, I never looked back. The atmosphere is thick with encouragement, motivation, ever-evolving challenges (both physical and mental), and the camaraderie from everyone, campers and instructors alike, is unmatched. I have dropped 14 pounds, seven inches, and three pant sizes. I now see muscles where I never knew they existed!
>
> —Josie

> When I started TROTFITNESS, I was completely out of shape. I started getting serious about boot camp and with the amazing training

and motivation I received from Nisan, I lost 22 pounds and 10 inches. Now I can fit back into my clothes. It feels like I have a whole new wardrobe with having to shop for smaller sizes.

—Carol

I just want TROTFITNESS to know how much they have influenced me at the ripe age of 40! I lost 26 pounds, seven inches, and five percent body fat in just 90 days. I love you guys for all you do and for the effort you put in every day to change people's lives. Thanks again!

—Chad

I came to TROTFITNESS frustrated, lacking motivation, and wanting to be more fit. I wasn't sure if TROT was going to be my cup of tea, but I thought to myself I have nothing to lose with the possibility of a boatload to gain. I don't regret the decision at all! The atmosphere is encouraging and I find that arrogance is absent in this program—a much welcomed bonus. I wanted to lose weight, lose inches, drop my cholesterol, and increase my fitness. I'm well on my way to achieving all those goals!

—Cindy

I can truly say without TROTFITNESS, I would not have been able to lose the extra weight. This is a life changing process!

—Dena

To think, it started with a decision. A decision to quit advanced my gift, mission, and calling. Now invitations to speak at some of the nation's biggest fitness conferences have been sent my way because of the success of TROTFITNESS. Wow. Glory to God. I have been given the opportunity to encourage many aspiring fitness professionals about my unique path into the industry. Their eyes light up with fire when they connect my ambition to quit to new possibilities of fun with my God-given gifts.

What great fortune to be able to vicariously live out my passion. I would not be here today without deciding to quit first. My time working with Bucknell gave me a wonderful platform to grow and go. I believe wisdom is the ability to acknowledge victorious pursuits versus vain pursuits. I'm winning because of the bravery to lay down an unfit cause for me to carry.

What will you quit today?

When I stopped holding on to a great job, my hands opened wide enough to clutch a phenomenal career. I eventually earned the 2015 Fitness Business Summit Personal Trainer of the Year Award. It was my time.

There's a time for everything. Am I saying drop what you are doing immediately even if it takes food out of your kid's mouth? Not a chance. Am I saying to walk away even though you have no options and the lights in your home will be cut off as a consequence? Absolutely not. "There is a time to plant and there is a time to uproot" (Ecclesiastes 3:2).

My prayer is for you to be sensitive to the time. There is a perfect opportunity awaiting you at the right time. Your gift is waiting for you to quit your willpower so you can give it proper attention. You cannot be at your very best on double duty trying to merely claim a paycheck and conquer your calling. My sincere hope is for you to have enough faith to believe the world is in dire need of your gift. Don't allow the residence of your gift to be in a holding chamber. Stop putting a standstill on what you were born to do. You need to quit so you can birth your gift.

Fill in Blanks

1. There is a boatload of profit to be made in _____.

2. There is a ____ for everything.

3. Sometimes, you have to notice when time has _____ and the _____ to quit is made available.

Chapter Challenge

Is there something you have been holding on to far too long? It may very well be time to let it go. Make an inventory of your valuables versus invaluable thoughts and get rid of the unnecessary. It's time to quit.

Chapter 11

MOVE OVER.
MY GIFT IS TOO BIG!

> If you set goals and go after them with all
> the determination you can muster, your gifts
> will take you places that will amaze you.
>
> — Les Brown

Dude/dudet, the size of your gift is ridiculously large. The expanse of your gift cannot be measured with the longest of yardsticks. Know this: when God gives you something, He doesn't go halfway. In fact, I don't think you realize the magnitude of your possession. It cannot fit in a box. There is not enough wrapping paper to cover it. Whether your dreams consist of teaching kids, feeding the hungry, flying airplanes, or engineering bridges, the gift inside you is so big everything else must move over.

The floodgates open wide for your gifts when they're no longer tied down by meaningless endeavors. Life simplifies when everything you see in the front-view mirror is the undeniable, massive potential of your gift. *Potential* is a word that should not be taken lightly. Society places a lot of stock in potential. Fortune 500 companies hire headhunters to recruit senior-level executives based on their potential to increase profit. The parents of little Susie invested in piano lessons because of the expressed interest of their daughter, who has the potential to develop her artistic side. Puppy stores are in business today because Fido and Lassie have the potential to make folks happier. If those scenarios have potential, then what about your gift?

Imagine the depth of your goodness when nothing else matters but growing your God-given abilities because of the potential therein? How far can they take you? I know it may sound a bit extreme—that is, having tunnel vision to focus on nothing but your gift when you have kids screaming in the background, a big mortgage to pay off, or a humming desire to embrace your nomadic side that wants to travel and see the world. However, daydream with me for one minute about the absolute delight of spending every waking second, minute, hour, and day locked into doing what you were born to do. What if you loved poetry? Would you like to fill your agenda with poetry-writing sessions, attending poetry slams, and learning from other artists? What if you loved veterinary science and began to fill your schedule by helping find cures for animals with diseases? I have a very strong feeling life would be sweeter all the more if you spent more time doing what you love.

There are not enough people in the world doing what they love to do. Read the following line out loud: "I will not spend my life doing what I hate." You felt empowered, right? Read it again. Sounds simple—I know. Yet why is it so hard to follow? Why aren't more people being adventurous with their lives, marching to the beat of their own drum? No one should sit on the bleachers when they can score on the playing field of their own life. My fellow gifted comrade, get up and start having fun like a kid again. Who told you to grow up and become a boring adult? Never. You have way too much potential. Now is the time to capitalize on it. Let me show you how.

There once was a little boy named Nelson whose love for basketball took off like a rocket. Once church let out, he would dart up to the house through the grassy Southern plains to catch his favorite basketball team on prime-time TV. He even saved allowance money to buy the best wall posters of basketball legends who were seen as gods in his eyes.

One night, while he was fast asleep, his parents pried open his bedroom door and sneaked in a regulation-size, burned-orange, grippy basketball for him (just like the pros). It was still in its box, spanking brand-new, fresh smell and all. They knew Nelson would see it first thing in the morning and be extremely happy. He's been asking for a basketball for weeks.

Once daylight crept through his room's curtains, waking Nelson up from his dreams, his parents' plan began to play out perfectly. Nelson spotted the roundball at the foot of his room door and let out a playful scream. Immediately, he jumped out of bed to squeeze, clutch, and hug his new gift. The two were inseparable.

Through the neighborhood he went, bouncing his new ball up and down the streets, and everyone watched in adoration. The ball would dribble off his foot into the ditches, and off went Nelson, quickly scampering after it to reclaim rightful possession. He was the first to admit he wasn't very good, but Nelson promised that one day, everyone will be watching him on TV and his poster will cover the bedroom walls of millions. Day after day, night after night, Nelson practiced and honed his skills as a player. Kids who started off their days playing by his side never outlasted him. They would turn in for bed or be interested in something else, and Nelson continued shooting hoops alone on the basketball court.

His parents figured this would be another one of those boyish fads and it would only be a matter of time before Nelson chased after other passions. They were wrong. From youth basketball to middle school, from summer league to high school, Nelson made every single practice and played in every single game, and you guessed it, he became a star.

Several of the top college recruiters around the nation attended his games, salivating for his talent. Nelson decided to be a stellar collegiate student athlete at the state college about five hours north of his hometown. His first semester of college was much harder academically than high school—more homework and group projects, tougher quizzes and exams. He had to spend less time playing ball and more time studying. To make matters worse, the girls on campus were calling for him. Jealous teammates only wished they had those types of problems. His handsome build and Southern charm made it very easy to catch a lady's eye. With the pressing demands of school lessons and a beautiful girlfriend beside him, his basketball stats took a significant dip. However, the story doesn't end the way you may think it's going.

Overtime, Nelson was still good enough to bounce back statistically and continue being the big man on campus throughout his remaining years of school. He found a way to balance and adjust to college life. His senior year finished with him leading the nation in steals, winning the conference championship, and even getting drafted to play in the big times. Signing on the dotted line of his pro contract was a dream come true. Everyone thought Nelson was great until they witnessed him play at the professional level. He went from great to phenomenal. You should have seen him. He was bigger, faster, and stronger. Nobody could stop what he wanted to do on the court. He had the sweetest jump shot. Those no-look passes for assist flooded his stats. He was even smarter on the court than his collegiate years, constantly making the right basketball decisions, to the pleasure of the coaching staff. He won a few championships and MVP league honors before retiring to live happily ever after.

Nelson goes down as one of the most gifted and decorated players to have ever touched a regulation-size, burned-orange, grippy basketball, one whose pro career far outshined his collegiate one.

Why didn't Nelson's story turn for the worse like you probably projected? How come he gets the "happily ever after" at the end? The answer is very simple. Of course, adjusting and balancing to his new life in college was a big step, but there is another story implied here. When Nelson turned pro, he was able to focus more time and attention on his gift. This is when his talent skyrocketed. He was already good at playing basketball, or at least good enough to garner the respect of scouts at the college and pro level.

However, when he went pro, he was able to really go pro! What I didn't share is the focused effort he dedicated in making more time to run sprints, do quick feet drills, and develop better passing abilities. He hired a shooting coach to help him perfect his jump shot from deep and a top-notch chef to help with his nutrition. Food became his fuel for success versus those greasy pizzas he scarfed down in college. You get the point, right? His gift was too big for him to focus on anything else other than being the best at what he was created to do—playing with the roundball. His life was structured around his passion, as opposed to his passion being structured around his life. Other things had to move over to make room for his gift.

Proverbs 18:16 says, "A man's gifts make room for him and brings him around great men" (NASV). Referencing back to chapter 7, he kept the main thing, the main thing. Now this isn't to say Nelson didn't have a life outside of his gift and the only thing he did was play basketball. My friend, don't miss the forest for the tree here. There is a major difference between commitment and crazy.

Commitment is dialing in, putting forth a consistent and concerted effort. Crazy is wearing yourself out and depleting your energy to the point you cannot perform, function, and even think straight. Nelson put his foot down and made a commitment. He committed to his commitment.

Did you know there is something you can go pro in as well? It's your gift! Make the decision today: like Nelson, look for resources to help you maximize the time you have with your gift. Let us remember, life is but a vapor. Nelson hired a shooting coach and chef. Who will you bring on board to be a coach or mentor? You need someone fully aware of your gift. And you need to work your craft so well others acknowledge how good you are.

Nelson had a stocked-out trophy mantle of awards and honors. He started off dribbling the basketball off his foot and into ditches. You too have to be willing to practice, embrace a strong work ethic, and master the mundane until your gift grows out of infancy into XL status.

Fill in the Blanks

1. The gift inside you is so big everything else must _____.

2. There are not enough people in the world doing _____.

3. Commitment is putting forth a _____. Crazy
   is _____ and depleting your energy to
   the point you cannot perform, function, and even think
   straight.

Chapter Challenge

Invest in a coach or mentor who will help you grow in your
gifting. It's time to go pro!

Chapter 12

FULFILL YOUR ASSIGNMENT

My assignment is to take my situation
and use it to help others who feel hopeless
and/or helpless because of loss.

—Marvin Sapp

Do you know whom you are assigned to? I know making lots of din-ero is an attractive lure. I know living in a fancy house with the nicely stained deck on back makes you drool. I'm not here to discourage those goals. However, more important than money in the bank or driving the latest luxury vehicle are the people assigned to your life.

For starters, people are your greatest asset. We need one another to survive. Jewelry, fine clothes, and expensive accessories can't buy someone's affection. At some point, you will need someone at some place at some time. Count on it.

In fact, there are three types of essential relationships you need to have established in your life. I refer to them as an upline, sideline, and downline.

Your upline may consist of advisers, mentors, and/or coaches. These are the people who are perhaps harder driven and smarter than you. It should be quite humbling to be in their presence because it requires you to think and be on your toes.

"As iron sharpens iron, so a friend sharpens the countenance of a friend" (Proverbs 27:17). How about using this verse as checks and balances for friendships? It raises the bar and sets higher standards.

If your friend isn't making you better, making you think, making you sharper, then maybe you should look for another one. You certainly do not have to be the dullest knife in the drawer when aligning yourself with others, but it's also not wise to be the sharpest tool in the shed either. Your learning will suffer. You will constantly be the one providing answers. May I suggest an upline? Seek out those who are willing to pour handsomely into your development, helping you grow in your special gifts and talents. Your upline makes a strong impression on you with the awe-inspiring work they have accomplished in life. You look up to them for a variety of reasons, namely because of the major contributions they have made among their communities, companies, and companions. You revere them as big-time change agents. They are the fearless leaders and trendsetters. Everyone is familiar with their work and holds them in high regard.

My pastor is one of several uplines in my life. Wisdom oozes from his pores. Proverbs 13:20 encourages to "walk with the wise and become wise, for a companion of fools suffers harm." I am wise for being simple and simply taking time out of my schedule to be around him. We meet once a month, and I do most of the listening. There is no big agenda other than to spend time with each other. He never fails to answer the hard questions plaguing my mind. He is indeed a man of integrity offering support and words of truth when needed most. Consider it wise to have multiple uplines of different kinds as well—teachers, parents, business leaders, strategists, and so on. The more the merrier. They ensure the success of your purposes and plans. "Plans fail for lack of counsel, but with many advisers they succeed" (Proverbs 15:22).

Let's briefly discuss your sideline now. Shoulder to shoulder they stand next to you. You coexist on the same level. You are on an equal playing field with your sidelines. It is the peer who is in the MBA program with you or the associate working alongside who earned the same promotion. This type of relationship is pivotal for the mutual exchange of ideas. You have great ideas to share with your sideline, which they can use for their own personal advancement. And you respect the information your sideline shares to help with your performance.

Sidelines make some of the best partners to breathe life into your gifting and vision. They have a similar focus, similar skill set, and similar trajectory. Sidelines scratch each other's back. They look out for each other. Back and forth they e-mail and text the latest tips of their industry or expertise. Sidelines have a very fun relationship, coupled with friendly competition to push each other and bring out the best in each other. When you witness your sideline aspire to greatness with their gift, it feels as though you are next in line because you had a hand in their success. Sidelines arrive to their destiny because of you, and you arrive to your destiny because of them.

Finally, the most important relationship among the three (in my opinion) is your downline. Folks in your downline make up your assignment. These relationships must be treated with a bit more care and concern than the others. Individuals in your downline pull and tug at your heartstrings because they absolutely need the best version of you.

Answer a couple of questions for me, please. Who needs you most right now? Who is your mentee? Downlines can be your beloved children, hired staff, or members of the charitable organization down the street.

A statement attributed to Buddha and the theosophists says, "When the student is ready, the master appears." While I am sure there is a lot of truth jam-packed in this statement, I believe otherwise: "When the teacher is ready, the student appears."

You are the teacher. But are you ready to teach, train, share, serve, cultivate, corral, impart, impress, drive, dedicate, coach, compose, galvanize, give, lift up, lead out, pour into, and press into the lives of those who are assigned to you?

Seek to bless your downline as if it were an honorable duty. See yourself as Special Ops military forces supplied with unique arsenal and weaponry to save the day for those in your downline. You have a core group of believers who need your gift and your message. They are waiting for you to do more and say more. If you were to sit on a big chair, then your downline would be positioned at your feet, clinging to every word of knowledge and wisdom shared. What a selfless way to live life. Do you agree? Do you trust your life's mission and core philosophy? It's your gift!

Don't devalue your sphere of influence or how to appeal to them. You bring a lot to the table, and your downline knows it, loves it, needs it. Put all the chips on the table. It's not a gamble when catering to your assignment. Although it may be tempting to discredit the power of your message and the potency of your gift, cast down the urge to do so because there's an attentive audience honored to listen and receive from you. They are drawn to you, and you can no longer ignore them. They are the people God has specifically put in your life so you can touch them in a special way.

Warning: I caution you not to be disheartened by those who leave your life when you begin speaking and living out what you were born to do. If they choose to walk away because of your decision to use your gift, their departure proves they were not assigned to you. Begin to make the distinction among people who come into your life for a reason, season, or lifetime. It's okay to let go of those who do not want or value what you have to offer. If necessary, show them the door out of your life. You may think this is rude, but keep in mind, you are opening a spot for someone else who appreciates your gift. Go where you are celebrated and not merely tolerated. Go to someone who would love to be a part of your downline, to be served by you, to be blessed by you.

There is no need to fight for territory in people's life. Your message and gift act like a magnet attracting those interested. Your responsibility is to know, in deep context, the specific calling you have to share. Whosoever values your gift may bathe in the goodness of it. You cannot be insensitive to those who come to you in appreciation versus those who are passersby. It will happen. In fact, your gift is not designed to serve everyone. No matter how good and beneficial, some will pass up what you have to offer. Although you may reach the level of sharing your gift on a worldwide platform, it doesn't mean everyone will embrace it with adoration. You will serve good, healthy food, but do not be surprised by those who would rather have the fatty goods. Again, people who go in the opposite direction simply are not assigned to you.

Your impact will fall elsewhere. Spend your efforts there. Give your gift generously there. Speak there. Les Brown says, "Never speak where you do not have a voice." Trying to influence those who either do not want to hear your voice or turn a deaf ear to it can feel like a lost cause. Preserve your good stuff for the downline. Matthew 7:6 instructs, "Do not cast your pearls before pigs." In other words, give your gift to those who will see it as a precious pearl. Protect yourself from haters or unappreciative folks who will publicly attack you on blogs, websites, and social media. If they prefer to waddle with your gift in the mud like a pig, they aren't assigned to you. Go to those who love your gift. Go to those who desire your pearls. These are your downline.

Finally, be careful not to confuse my choice of word, *downline*, as folks who are beneath you. No. These are people high on your priority list. As you assist in their change and continue to pour into their cup, get ready for your cup to overflow. You will experience much love and joy from your downline and come to regard their transformative stories as priceless.

Let's focus: You need an upline, sideline, and downline. Each plays a key role in fulfilling your assignment.

Fill in the Blanks

1. There are three types of essential relationships you need to have established in your life. I refer to them as an _____, _____, and _____.

2. I also believe, "when the _____ is ready, the _____ appears." You are the teacher.

3.   Go to those who desire your _____.

Chapter Challenge

People come into your life for a reason, season, or lifetime. Assess the relationships in your life right now and categorize them in one of the three: upline, downline, or sideline.

Chapter 13

IT'S A WAR ZONE

A mind is a terrible thing to waste.

—Arthur Fletcher

Please do not wrestle mentally with yourself any longer. I am calling a time-out from the battle wreaking havoc on your untapped potential. Why are you questioning whether you have "it" or not? Please note: everyone has what I like to call the "it" factor. However, each individual must dive into the deep waters of their own life to discover precious jewels about themselves. You see, there aren't enough people willing to self-examine themselves in quest to find their "it."

Socrates said, "The unexamined life is not worth living." However, when you search to discover yourself in a brand-new way, life comes alive. The crazy thing is, you don't have to look too hard to find your "it." Take some time to meditate on what makes you different and unique. Figure out what matters to you the most. Be willing to ask yourself questions like "What do I really care about?" "What gets me fired up?" "What are my big interests?" Interrogate yourself. Then make a list of the answers. The items on this list make your "it" factor, and sometimes they cannot be described in words. Yet when you see a person operating in their "it," you catch yourself saying, "They just have *it*."

For instance, let's take a look at Eddie Holman, American singer and recording artist of the hit single from the 1970s "Hey

There Lonely Girl." My wife and I watched him sing live in concert at sixty-eight years of age. That's right, sixty-eight. Eddie was singing those high notes to the high heavens. He sounded like a bird onstage. We could have thought it was very hard to sing at Eddie's age because of the physical demands placed on his vocal cords, but think again. It wasn't only his singing; his charisma and stage presence captivated the audience, and it was unprecedented. We were in the palms of his hands. "Eddie has 'it,'" I murmured in my wife's ear as we listened in awe. In fact, he makes "it" look quite easy. He is what you call a natural. Eddie shared from the stage that he has been in show business for over forty years; no wonder he was so good at operating in his "it." You don't question for once what this guy was meant to do: sing!

Now this is Eddie. What about you?

Maybe you have been in awe of others far too long at the risk of ignoring what makes you the real deal. I want you to spend some necessary "me time" and figure out how to get in tune with yourself. Shakespeare said, "To thine own self be true." Unfortunately, many people have settled for the lie that whispers nasty nothings into their ears. The ears are the gateway to the mind. Significant damage is threatening the bright future of your gift because either you have heard or believed you're not good enough or you are just like any other average Jane or Joe or you have been told to take a hike, sit in the backseat, and watch those with a real gift shine because you're a fraud. What garbage!

It's time to eliminate the waste of the mind. Bad thoughts don't belong near you, so put them in the dumpster instead. From this point forward, you must repeatedly think, *I am born gifted.* Be true to your convictions even if it calls for reaching deep down within yourself to grasp them. Your convictions, as opposed to those nasty nothings, sound like the following: "I have what it takes to make it," "I'm a hidden gem," "The world has not seen my best stuff," "One day, I am going to shout like the great Muhammad Ali, 'I shocked the world!' Come on now, these are your gut feelings, and you and I both know it. God does not create junk, so why has your mind become a safe place to harbor negative thoughts?

Your mind can become the greatest asset for your gifting or the biggest liability. You are in control. Are you taking inventory of your thoughts? Track them, monitor them, and access what you constantly think about.

Imagine your mind has eyeballs. Now use your mind's eyes to think of positive outcomes. Picture yourself making the best choices for your greatest success. Your mind's eyes can foreshadow you eating the healthy snacks at the upcoming holiday party. Your mind's eyes can forecast you turning in the work assignment well before the deadline. Your mind's eyes can even project living in the palace of your dreams, owning multiple businesses, and fulfilling the needs of those you have always wanted to serve. Your mind's eyes are limitless.

Close your eyes right now and begin to think and see perfect outcomes for your coming attractions.

I hope you are overweight in positivity. When dirty dishes start to flood the kitchen sink, a bad odor begins to permeate through the entire home. Such is the case with your mind. When negative thoughts take residence in your mind, your entire life starts to stink. Your thoughts have the power to turn your gift into a beautiful manifestation of God's greatness, so allow them. Give your thoughts permission to manufacture the best you possible. The worst thing you can do is harbor toxic thoughts about yourself. This ruins the momentum toward doing what you were born to do. Your gift deserves better. Who cares if you are not the very best? Commit to getting better. Sing more. Write more. Give more. Lead more. Motivate more. Then follow it all by saturating yourself with beautiful thoughts.

Can you see it now? You magnify the power of your gifting with big, bold thoughts. Small thinking lands you nowhere. Your wildest imagination and biggest dreams are not imaginative and big enough. Go bigger. Your mind has no cap on it. So take the limits off. Throw the shackles away.

David gives indication of God's overwhelming thoughts toward you and me in Psalms 139:17-16. It reads, "How precious are your thoughts about me, O God. They cannot be numbered. I cannot even count them, they outnumber the grains of sand!" Ridiculous!

Did you catch it? There is not enough math in the world to factor up the amount of good thoughts God has about us. So why waste time thinking poorly? Pad your gifts and their abilities with the thoughts of God. Societal drama and negative people are going to violently bump into you, so protection on each side is very much needed.

Your shield against such forces is found within your mind, which is why your mind should focus on the quote below:

"Whatever things are true, whatever things are honest, whatever things are just, whatever things are pure, whatever things are lovely, whatever things are of good report; if there be any virtue, and if there be any praise, think on these things." (Philippians 4:8).

I was about three rows back, to the left of center stage, at my first ever hugely attended Fitness Business Summit (FBS) event in Costa Mesa, California. One of my best buddies hooked me up with some discounted tickets, so I was thrilled to be in the building. Every presenter who graced the platform was magical as they shared tips on how to be a successful fitness entrepreneur. Many even made their stories personal. They divulged amazing strategies on how to over-come fear and rid yourself of the crabs in life who try to pinch and pull you down. I quickly noticed that the fitness conference was less about fitness and more about personal development. My eyes were glued to seeing the best in our industry do their thing, but my mind began to wander off from time to time. When I drifted off, it was like an out-of-body experience as I daydreamed about next year's FBS event. I envisioned myself passionately speaking on the same stage with authority, spunk, and energy. It did not stop there.

I realized the host awarded a shiny, glassy Personal Trainer of the Year Award. My mind could not help but foreshadow that one day, I would be holding the same hardware above my head. My thoughts were pretty vivid, and greater thoughts continued to overtake me. My wife could not attend the conference with me at the time; the expenses were too much to fly both of us across the country. We conservatively made the decision for her to remain at home while I attended. However, while at the event, here goes my mind toying with big thoughts again: *Next time I'm at FBS, my wife will be right next to me because money will not be an issue.*

Low and behold, everything I imagined took place the following year. I humbly and dynamically presented from stage at FBS '15. The title of my message was "Why You Need a Heart Transplant to Grow a Massively Successful Fitness Business." I discussed how important it is, as a business owner, to have a fearless heart in your endeavors and how sacred it is to have a generous heart toward your clients and local community. My speech won the Best Presenter Award. Also, cheers from a gigantic audience came my way when I was announced winner of the FBS '15 Personal Trainer of the Year Award. Among the crowd's massive noise of cheers, I could pick out my wife's excitement in her yelling and screaming. She was so proud to be by my side and witness it all. It was her award too!

Be thankful for the blessings that accompany a big, beautiful imagination. "As a man thinketh, so is he" (Proverbs 23:7).

Living in massive success takes more thought than you may realize. Have fun with the practice of stretching your mind to think big. Why not? God has gifted you with an imagination, so use it. Dare I say your biggest thoughts are small in God's mind eyes. He wants to challenge you to believe in the amazing thoughts of your mind, to which He has the unfathomable power to make reality. He is the ultimate Gift Giver who wants to embrace a mind-set willing to test the capabilities of His mighty hand. He says, "So, Nisan, you want to be a fitness trainer? How about Personal Trainer of the Year? You want to speak at Fitness Business Summit? How about being honored with the Best Presenter Award?"

Be willing to add the extra onto your big thoughts because you can handle it. Use your mind to conquer the impossible. Do not waste its potential. By thinking wonderfully, you will survive in the war zone of your mind.

Fill in the Blanks

1. Each individual must dive into the deep waters of their _____ to discover precious jewels about themselves.

2. The worst thing you can do is harbor _____ about yourself.

3. He is the ultimate Gift Giver who wants to embrace a _____ willing to test the capabilities of his mighty hand.

Chapter Challenge

Practice the habit of taking your big thoughts to the next level all week. Push yourself to think bigger and bigger and bigger! Do you desire to earn a college degree? If so, think about earning two of them or finishing school a year early. Your mind's eyes are limitless.

Chapter 14

WORK YOUR GIFT

All roads that lead to success have to
pass through Hard Work Boulevard.

—Eric Thomas

Imagination is awesome, but having your head high in the clouds without taking massive action on your thoughts will lead to a dead end each time. Big thoughts may cause you to feel good for a moment, but they are not good enough to last or sustain you. There will be a void and emptiness in life if the only thing you have to show for your ideas are your ideas. You want to feel, touch, and grab your dreams, not simply allow them to exist in outer space. So it's imperative you roll up your sleeves now, pound the pavement, put in the extra time, and get to work. The future of your gift heading to the highest of mountaintops depends on your willingness to take massive action.

Massive action is not for the faint of heart, my friend. Those two words combined mean a whole lot and should not be glossed over. You have to start by taking action first. Trust me. I know the obvious is being stated, but many people struggle to be action takers, let alone massive action takers. They see what they want but lack the get-up-and-go mentality. They are comfortable propping their feet up on the sofa and folding their arms behind the head, saying, "Tomorrow is a new day. I will address my agenda then!" They leave office work on the table for the next day when it could have been completed eons ago. Rarely, if ever, do they say, "I'll do it now." They would much rather shove responsibilities over in someone's lap while enjoying coworkers near the watercooler. These are nonaction takers.

Instead, you are among the 10 percent of the world population who does not complain about their to-do list. On the contrary, you embrace the marching orders for the day with pride. You recognize that griping about workload does not go far in life. The joke is, 80 percent of people in this world do not listen to complaints and the other 20 percent are glad it's you.

Born Gifted is igniting your switch because you have a very sensitive beast-mode button; press at a moment's notice. You are taking action this very moment by reading powerful content and allowing it to marinate in your system. And you are not stopping at the marinating stage. You are soaking up the information in *Born Gifted* so you can apply everything learned, and later you'll squeeze all the juices out of what has been gathered. Your gift is on the line. You know if there is a trace of your gift drying up or fizzling out, then taking massive action will resuscitate it back to life.

You have the power to breathe life into your gift. You don't have to be a magician to create your own magic. A powerful pastor by the name of Timothy reminded his followers in 2 Timothy 1:6, "For this reason, I remind you to fan into flames the gift of God, which is in you through the laying on of my hands."

First, you may be thinking, *I've never been touched by Timothy*. While you are correct, remember, God has His hands on you right now—far better, far more powerful. Because of this truth, feel empowered to fan or rekindle the gift resting inside you. May it be a bright, burning flame because God is with you.

Fanning underscores the significance of putting in the work to start your own fire. Sometimes, it takes a little reminding from others to understand you have a special gift waiting to shine. I'm your reminder!

Have you ever had to use a handheld fan to keep cool? Because I grew up in an old-school black Southern church in Alabama with no air-conditioning, I know the importance of cardboard hand fans. The ushers, wearing white gloves, used to hand them to the congregation like porcelain gifts. As one stoically sits, in escalating temperatures, listening to the pastor's sermon, stillness wasn't enough to keep the beads of sweat from forming on the forehead. But then came the cardboard fan with the wooden stick at the end ready to serve as a personal cooling device. It was imperative to stroke the fan across slightly in front of the face, as fast as possible, to conjure up the smallest of breezes. The small fan literally felt like it was saving your life from the surrounding heat.

Do you see where I'm going now?

When you fan, the gift inside you rises. Imagine your gift becoming better than a cool breeze. Real effort must be put forth to "fan into flames," but the ramifications spell your comfort, peace, joy, and survival. Fanning addresses the ability to be productive. The air from your fan brings life to your gift. Please note: a lack of action smothers the potential of what you have inside you; it takes the oxygen away. So what are you going to do about it?

Take massive action, of course.

Massive action entails doing whatever is necessary, whatever it takes (ethically, of course) to stand out with your gift. I'm not talking about sporadic check-ins, working hard when the boss is looking then hardly working when he/she turns their back. No. Massive action means you are kicking Mr. Lazy to the curb.

Procrastination should also be strangled because of your hustle. Massive action is the proof that you want it bad, real bad. You detest those who are all talk and no action. In the words of NFL running back Marshawn Lynch, you're "'bout that action boss."

Imagine phone calls made, e-mails answered, blog postings uploaded, new video content released, and it's all finished without missing a step. You are dancing freely with your gift. You work with purpose on things that really matter in order to not merely do busy work for the sake of looking good. You are no longer a rookie; you are a pro. Marking through agenda items doesn't satisfy you or make you happy. Instead, marking through the right agenda items puts a smile on your face. Hard work and dedication should be your first and last name because settling isn't an option.

Refuse to be one of those talented people who never work, who rest on their laurels. Refuse to lie dormant when your gifting begs your attention. Refuse to allow the 206 bones in your body to have a lazy-bone companion. Eric Thomas, in his book *The Secret to Success*, wrote, "All roads that lead to success have to pass through Hard Work Boulevard."

I know you are talented. I am certain many praise your God-given abilities. Yet you still need lifelong priorities and deep focus. Ascend to greatness. Level up and contend toward the next level. Do you want to confidently look into the mirror with excitement and be proud of the efforts you have put toward your gift?

Executing your gift with precision to impact others does not translate to giving your average. It means working to be phenomenal. Healthy thoughts about your gift and future are a great place to start, but following through and finishing the job takes good old-fashioned work ethic.

For about two years, I wanted to accomplish an awesome physical transformation and compete in my first NPC Physique Competition. Yes. Two years. I was late to being stage ready with the chance to strut my stuff in board shorts. I had thoughts of newly defined abs, thoughts of boulder shoulders, thoughts of bulging biceps, but that was it.

Two calendar years passed by, leaving me saturated with big thoughts of competing. I had nothing to tangibly show for my ideas. Therefore, I wasted 730 days on a dream when I had every opportunity to put my thoughts into action.

Fortunately, I moved out of stagnancy, procrastination, laziness, or whatever else you want to name it; I stepped into taking massive action. My thoughts were the catalyst pushing me to compete; however, taking real action got me ready for my first spray tan and posing routine for a few hundred spectators while they judged my body composition. My chest did not grow bigger until I hit the bench press machine. Oh, what a journey it was! I see why the all-time great, eight-time Mr. Olympia Ronnie Coleman jokes, "Everybody wants to get big, but nobody wants to lift the heavy weights."

I embarked upon the biggest physical challenge of my entire adult life. Never had I worked out so consistently and so hard. Training two times a day became the norm. I was burning up the calories and building up muscles six days a week, Monday through Saturday. My cardio routine of running on the treadmill, gliding on the elliptical, or pedaling on the stationary bike started early mornings. Sometimes, I felt like a drained zombie on those machines, but it was important for me to put in the work to get the results. My weight training routine typically took place in the early evenings. The gym became my second home. My gift of encouragement was kicked into overdrive, and I would tell myself over and over again, "You can do this, Nisan. Don't give up. It will get better. Stay the course."

There were days I felt like throwing in the towel, but a transformation was happening in me. I could sense it. This kept me going.

In the beginning of my journey, I felt like a Thoroughbred racehorse running in the Kentucky Derby. Within the first eight weeks of physique competition training, I banged out a whopping eighty-eight workouts. While the most consistent gym-goers averaged three workouts per week, I was at the gym eleven times within a six-day stretch. I felt untouchable. Before you interpret my words as lofty bragging, please understand I'm not trying to impress you but rather impress upon you the value of taking massive action.

Changes were happening physically and mentally, and I loved it. Unfortunately, steam started letting out of my ship as I continued on the road to being physically fit. My progress was not quite what I desired within the twelve-week period of time. To say I underestimated the task, twice, is an understatement. One, I underestimated how much work it took to compete as a physique competitor. Two, I underestimated how much time it took to be stage ready. What I initially planned to be a twelve-week process actually took over a year.

Do you see the correlation between massively acting to accomplish my goals as a physique competitor and what it will take to excel in a gift?

You may be talented and receiving a lot of attention from admirers already, but to be your very best, you need to invest more action. Be a big-action taker. Also, allow time to take its course. Yep. Here comes the patient jargon. Some of your most important goals will take you the longest amount of time to obtain. If you could be there in a flash, then you would have a whole lot of company waiting for your arrival. Everyone would be the greatest if there wasn't a waiting game. Focus on this: work your gift and monitor the progress over time.

I was in decent shape prior to those two-a-day workouts. Nevertheless, to be in the greatest shape of my life, I had to celebrate my progress (big or small) over an extended period of time. Humbly placing top 10 of the NPC Lehigh Valley Championships for Men's Physique is now one of the grand highlights of my life; never to be forgotten. I worked my butt off, literally. The end results cannot be denied. As compared to when I started, I had a tighter midsection and broader shoulders, and dropped nearly 10 percent body fat. The lessons I learned through the experience can help anyone, whether they want to lose five pounds or one hundred pounds.

For my 10 Flabby-to-Firm Transformation Tips go to www. nisantrotter.com/borngifted. You will see a fitness icon. Click it for my fantastic tips and National Physique Competition transformation photos. Enjoy!

Fair warning for anyone who wants to rally around their biggest dreams: massive action is required.

Fill in the Blanks

1.   The chance of your gift reaching the mountaintop depends or your willingness to take _____.

2.   Marking through the _____ agenda items puts a smile on your face.

3. Executing your gift with precision to make a real impact on others does not mean work to be _____. It means work to be _____.

4. Ronnie Coleman jokes, "Everybody wants to get ____, but nobody wants to lift the ____ weights."

Chapter Challenge

Write down your biggest priorities needed in order to excel in your gift. Who are the people you need to connect with this week? Make a list of phone calls that must be made. Plan the trip. Send out the handwritten letters. Develop your massive-action to-do list and get it done!

Chapter 15

LIVE CREATIVE

Creative isn't the way I think.
It's the way I like to live.

—Paul Sandip

Do me a favor: if you believe or say the words "I'm just not that creative," then never believe or say them again. It is critical you hear me
out on this for the advancement of your gift. The more you believe or
say something, the more power you give that something (no matter
what it is). If you believe you're fat, then get ready to see a few extra
pounds on the scale or feel the blue jeans fitting tighter than usual. If
you say things like "I'm so stupid. I'm a dummy. I have no common
sense," then be prepared to live the reality of what you are speaking.

Both your thoughts and words have magnetic power. They
attract and attach to you, whether for good or bad, which is why
it is undeniably important to be careful what you think and say.
It's easy to speak demotivating words. In fact, I believe many don't
realize when they do it. In similar fashion, it's simple to believe the
self-sabotaging thoughts roaming in your head, without being fully
aware of their presence. Going forward, I want you to think from
an entirely different vantage point. Consider life's possibilities if you
conditioned your mind to think creatively on a regular basis. Where
would you be if creative thinking was an unshakeable habit?

For starters, allow me to inform that your creative genes are
already at work. You simply haven't been paying attention to them.

How many times have you reworked your busy schedule to squeeze in some time with a close friend? Creativity at work. What about the variety of weekend plans you come up with to keep life interesting? Creativity at work. The countless ways you mix and match the same sets of clothes in your wardrobe, so much so folks believe you have a millionaire budget. Creativity at work. What about the plethora of fun photos overriding the SIM card of your smartphone? Again, creativity at work.

God made human beings innately creative, and we can grow with more intentionality. Take for instance Adam in the garden of Eden; he was one-on-one with God before Eve ever stepped on the scene. One of his first assignments is found in Genesis 2:19: "So the Lord God formed from the ground all the wild animals and all the birds of the sky. He brought them to the man to see what he would call them. And the man chose a name for each one." Before Adam's creativity was put to work in naming the wild animals and birds, their names were…well…wild animals and birds. God tasked Adam with naming every creature we know today, a very tall order.

I imagine an endless assembly line of animals stretched across the vast prairie. One by one, flying fowl by flying fowl, animal by animal, Adam engaged his creative thoughts to pronounce a new name for each one. Now I don't know how many animals existed way back then, but online arguments state that it ranged from two million to fifty million; some say ten thousand species of new animals were discovered every year. Also, an estimated ten-thousand-plus birds graced the sky alone. So here Adam stood, fairly fresh to the world, and said, "I'll call you Zebra. You will be known as Robin. Let's go with Chicken for you. Lion, Deer, Turkey, Elephant, Chimpanzee (that's a fun name)…"

Be encouraged. Your ability to create is larger than the credit given. You have the power to create new ideas, new stories, new concepts, and even new versions of how to use your gift. Steve Jobs used his creative thinking for Apple. Mark Zuckerberg crafted Facebook. How creative will you not only think but also live? What can you do with your gift that has never been done? Stretch your mind. Come up with a new efficient way. Develop a new niche. Carve out a new space. Everything has not been thought. All the good ideas have not been taken. Why? Because you haven't thought of one yet! In fact, the next big idea is waiting on you. Only you have the creative juices to fill the cup of your new adventure. Ask yourself constantly "Am I getting the most out of what I was born to do, or is there something else, something new I should be doing?" Be your own explorative think tank for conjuring up new ideas (as it concerns your gift).

You don't need a whole lot of money for research and development to make this happen. Pull out a scratch pad and pencil; jot down what first comes to mind. I don't believe we, as creative people made from a creative God, brainstorm enough.

We don't challenge our ability to think outside the box enough. We make creative thinking harder than necessary when it actually comes out naturally. We feel like it's magical when somebody is operating in the newness of their ideas, yet our everyday lives should also be engulfed in creativity.

Look, I want to provide you with more than just a "be creative" pep talk, so here's where you should start, especially as it concerns your gift:

First, believe you have something inside of you that has never been seen or done before. Believe you have special powers. Believe you are a superhero in your own right, uniquely equipped with a resistance to following the status quo. Someone you revere and respect may already be functioning at a world-class level in the same gift you were born to display. And it may feel as though they beat you to the punch and arrived first. However, how you shine and deliver your goods will be completely different because there is only one you.

Study what the greats have done and use their efforts to catapult forward. Your ideas can be the edited version. The fun part: You both can be great! You both can win! So there is no need for jealousy, envy, backbiting, or foul play. Be confident at your core.

After starting with your belief, put faith into action by speaking aloud what your heart is experiencing. Open up the floodgate (your mouth) for positive words to flow through and describe how precise and creative you will employ your gift. Verbal affirmations trigger success. "There is life in the power of the tongue" (Proverbs 18:21). Magnify the fruitfulness of life by speaking and living creatively.

I have an exercise for you. Windex-clean your bedroom mirror to clearly see your reflection. Now stare into your eyes day and night while proclaiming the following: "I was born to create! New and fresh ideas on how to use my gift bombard my mind. I simply need to pay attention and execute them." Boom. There goes your affirmation to memorize and speak into existence. Feel free to play around with it by changing the words and making it your own. Take ownership of this practice. You can do it! Get ready for new ideas to come to you.

Also, hang around creative people. If you don't have any in your life, then find them. Their habits will rub off on you. The more you watch and listen to them, the more you learn how to grow your creative genes. They may be able to add more layers onto what you are thinking and make it better.

I guarantee there is another way to work your gift. Whether it is playing an instrument, coaching a client, or building a fence, if you spend enough time focusing on how to be new and different, the ideas will come. Be patient enough to wait and see what pops up.

My uncles from Alabama are fantastic, blue-collar men. They get it from their retired dad, my Paw Paw, was a jack-of-all-trades when it came to his work. As a farmer who grew vegetables in mass quantities and raised pigs, chickens and cows, Paw Paw did everything. He hauled loads of dirt in a dusty, humongous orange dump truck. He also built some of the longest privacy fences you would ever want to see around plush green properties in the Land of the Beautiful. If there was a deck that needed to be added onto the house, a barn that needed a new tin roof, or even a deep-pit smoker -grill that needed to be welded, Harvey Mitchell (Paw Paw) did it with his bare, callused hands. He would wake up, dark and early, before everyone else to live out what he loved.

Blue-collar work was his gift, and there was absolutely nobody on the face of the earth happier doing what they were born to do. It was his pride and joy to take his boys (my uncles) along with him as he worked. They were big-time help to him, and he paid handsomely for their services—teaching them the ins and outs of the trade.

Before they were concrete, landscape, and fence builder entrepreneurs, it was Paw Paw who taught them everything they know. I absolutely loved working alongside Paw Paw and even my hardworking uncles. I marveled at how hard they worked and how easy it looked for them to fix problems. Talk about creativity and doing things their way; my Paw Paw and uncles never batted an eye at a crisis on the job. They would slow down for a minute or two, study and assess the damage, then they would screw in the board correctly, dig the hole properly, cut the tree down with safety, as if it weren't a big deal from the start.

Aside from Paw Paw, who carried the torch, how are my uncles so creative and so good? Well, they studied under Paw Paw before they ever had a name in town. They watched him come up with his own version of creativity, executing with great detail while on the job to ensure work was done right. Much like the blue-collar legacy Paw Paw left behind in the fields of Alabama, today my uncles can do anything out there with their own creative ingenuity.

When you know your gift and study those who creatively use it, get ready to fix, reinvent, and come up with your own way. The adventure is on!

Fill in the Blanks

1. Consider life's possibilities if you _____ your mind to think creatively on the _____.

2. You have the power to create new ideas, new stories, new concepts, and even new versions of _____.

3. We make creative thought harder than necessary when it truly comes _____.

Chapter Challenge

Once awake and before bedtime, repeat the affirmation for the next seven days: "I was born to create! New and fresh ideas on how to use my gift bombard my mind. I simply need to pay attention and execute them." And again, feel free to reword or creatively come up with your own affirmation.

Chapter 16

GIFT RESTORATION

A setback is a setup for a comeback.

—Willie Jolley

The creative juices flowing around the evolution of your gift are not enough to stop life from happening. Life's job is to get in the way and test what we're made of. From poor to rich, dumb to wise, there is no escape from having a hardship or two in this thing called life, no matter who you are or claim to be.

My sweet grandmother has a saying, "If you haven't had any problems, just keep living."

Will you crumble or wilt under pressure? Is the fire going to be too hot to bear? What happens to our DNA when the dreaded e-mail hits the inbox, when the life-changing voice message gets left on the cell phone, or the eviction letter drops in the mailbox? No one is immune from letting their mind wander with ruminating critical questions, such as "What would I do if this happened to me?" "Would I respond differently than others going through such traumatic experiences?" "How would I perform underneath so much turmoil?"

When adversity comes in like a raging storm, jeopardizing the survival of your gift, I wish it were easy to sell the "ride off into the sunset" story. Both you and I know better to believe the box office scripts made by Hollywood suggesting everyone wins.

There are winners and losers. You've seen it pan out too many times before in the lives of folks who apparently have the secrets to success, versus those who keep getting stung by failure and defeat. Heck, maybe you've even had a few life-altering losses. Now you fear the next one coming will be the straw that breaks the camel's back. Do you think about being TKOed by life? Is your gift drowning under the weight of trying to succeed in a burden-ridden world? If so, then you will love the words of Willie Jolley. He believes a "setback is a setup for a comeback." I have to agree with him.

Fresh out of my mother's womb, both of my legs were turned inward, both feet folded tight. I was deemed a crippled child. So for the better part of nine months, Mom carted me back and forth from my home in Silverhill, Alabama, across the bay to Mobile, where the closest crippled-child clinic resided. Not even one year old, I was given exercises so my legs and feet would function normally. Mom said the doctor's initial recommendation to fix my infancy problems was to break both legs. She refused to follow suit. She said it would be too crushing of a blow to witness her firstborn son with broken legs. Thankfully, Mom's stubbornness led doctors to apply two corrective casts instead.

They covered my feet and stopped just short of my kneecaps. Apparently, I hated them. At three months old—*bang bang, bang bang*—I was hitting and clanging the floors and walls. My baby legs were crying for freedom. In amazement, Mom saw me break out of those hard casts like the Incredible Hulk busting out of his tight T-shirt. My mother had to take me back to the clinic to get my casts fixed a number of times.

Eventually, the casts were taken off, and next up were these hideous-looking, corrective snow-white shoes with a straight bar between them. They sternly pressed my legs outward, and when barefoot, Mom aggressively massaged the insoles of my feet with her thick thumbs. I was too young to remember, but I can envision Mother wide-eyed with determination, pupils dialed-in with focus, pressing my little feet and mumbling, "Pshhh. Break my baby's legs. They must think I'm crazy."

At nine months, I was taking my first awkward baby steps. Both feet were turned outward as I tiptoed around only to fall on my soft bottom countless times. It would seem as if the corrective shoes were a bit much in straightening my lower extremities because kids in school said I walked like a duck. Their ridicule nearly ate me alive. Today when I reflect, I think, if they only knew my history, then I would have been serenaded with rounds of applause with every step.

However, overtime, my disability and disadvantageous legs became my competitive edge. They were crooked to begin, but God restored them to power. He used the boldness of my mom to ignore the physician's call to break them and start over. "No thank you!" I hear Mom saying. "We'll work with what we have."

As time continued to pass and my legs developed more strength, outrunning my competitors in sports became normal. Who would have expected that a child born with bowed legs and folded feet would richly excel in sports and be admired by his peers for his speed and quickness? I played Little League baseball, basketball, and football year-round. My teams were either first place or at the top of the league, and I had a lot to do with it. Teammates saw me as their leader. I made every all-star appearance and garnered lots of shiny trophies to put on top of the bedroom dresser. To think I could not have accomplished these feats if my legs remained in the same condition from birth. This is resounding evidence; you can start off on the wrong foot or, dare I say, wrong legs and still end up in the right place.

God is a restorer. In fact, this is one of His many characteristics. You might be feeling abandoned, down, out, hopeless when it comes to what was lost. You lost your mojo. You lost your fight. You lost the aspiration to skyrocket with your gift and do what you were born to do. If this is you, then I have some powerful words for you: believe in God's restorative power.

Jeremiah 30:17 says, "For I will restore health to you and your wounds. I will heal declares the Lord" (ESV). *Restore*, by definition, means to "bring back." My friend, because God is declaring He will restore health to you and your wounds or, in other words, bring you back—stop carrying the heavy load of worry, insecurity, and doubt. Take a massive dump; pun intended. The weight is far too heavy to shoulder. Put it all into the hands of the Lord. He is more than capable of carrying the weight and restoring what has been lost.

Oddly enough, I beg you to pause from thinking about what you are going to gain in life and start reminiscing about what you lost. God's getting ready to recover your ambition, recover your dreams, recover your drive, recover your joy and hope, recover your self-esteem, and recover your most prized possession that was lost in the shuffle of life. Once He recoups it, thankfully, He is not going to stop there. He is going to bring it back stronger than when it left. He delights in restoration!

Fill in the Blanks

1. Willie Jolley says, "A setback is a setup for a _____."

2. *Restore*, by definition, means _____.

Chapter Challenge

Reminisce about what you lost and believe God for restoration. Say a quick but powerful prayer on restoration right now.

Chapter 17

A DIFFERENCE IN BELIEF

Whether you think you can or
think you can't, you're right!

—Henry Ford

Allow me to draw and dig a deep line in the sand. There are those who believe they are supernaturally gifted and those who do not. Period. Some truly believe their God-given gifts, traits, and attributes are meant to set the world ablaze. And some merely think their purpose in life is to suck up earth's oxygen. Regardless of who you are and what you believe, comprehend this one truth: you believe in something.

Henry Ford, inventor of the model T-Ford, said, "Whether you think you can or think you can't, you're right." The goal of this chapter is to test your belief system. Do you really, really believe you are gifted? Do you believe it in your heart of hearts, deep in your knower? If the answer is yes, then how big are you winning?

In the game of basketball, some teams win just barely at the buzzer, off a whim, on hope, and on a prayer. The basketball is flying high in the air toward the hoop, and their hearts are racing because winning or losing is in the foreseeable future. Other teams, however, enjoy a blowout margin of victory—winning by twenty or thirty points. There is no question in the outcome. Take a guess on how I want you to win. Blowout, baby!

There should be no doubt that you are gifted. You are alive on this side of the ground where the grass grows, the flowers bloom, the round sun rises, the cars roam, and the houses get built stories high. I could stop here and say this is all the convincing you need to believe you are gifted. But think about this: if your purpose of existence were already fulfilled in the universe, if your gift could shine no brighter, then there would be no need for you. Ouch. Crazy thinking, huh?

Given the fact you are a breathing, functional human being, may I suggest that more goodness and giftedness has got to come out of you? Your time is not up when it comes to making a tremendous impact. Believe it. I hope you are not wrestling with this truth. You don't want self-limiting beliefs about your gifts and abilities to win. As you pace toward the end of *Born Gifted*, you should know by now, there is something special about you that many will pay homage to. My words would have turned you off many, many chapters ago had you not believed there was at least an inkling of awesomeness in you. Because you have landed on chapter 17, it's time to grow up even more. A fire should light in your eyes anticipating the testing of your belief system. Is the belief in your gift on a micro or macro level? It's time to find out. You can only be in one of two categories, believer or nonbeliever. I am making it as plain as pound cake for you. Let's go!

The Investment

Believers make investments in their gifts, dreams, and ambitions. The key word is *investment*. They refuse to see the expenditure of time, money, energy, or any other resource as an expense or waste when it comes to their dreams. Believers salivate at the ROI (return on investment), constantly believing they're onto something very big. They value their calling and invest in its potential, which in turn places their gift in another level.

On the other hand, nonbelievers walk around with clenched fists. They are unwilling to invest or even weigh the possibilities of success that could follow the slightest down payment. The cost of time is too expensive. After calculating the risk of putting in the energy and effort, nonbelievers backpedal in total skepticism, denying any possibilities that their gift has a shot. Excuses surface wildly like weeds among nonbelievers, and they use the scapegoat "I have no money." They ignore the fact many well-established entrepreneurial ventures today were built off angel investors, Go Fund Me, and so on. They are blind to the value of investing in their gift.

The Language

Those who believe in their gift possess an enthusiastic type of language that is foreign nowadays. They repeatedly say sentences like "I'm pumped!" "I'm thrilled!" "I cannot wait!" "This is going to be awesome!" Positivity rolls off the tongue of the believer. Excitement fills the room every time they speak about their gift. The language used by believers is motivating and empowering. You feel charged listening to them talk about what they want to do with their life. They speak loud. They talk up. They say it from their chest! In fact, hearing believers talk about what they were born to do inspires others to press the gas on their goals.

On the other hand, nonbelievers speak the common language of the land. Everyone has heard it too many times before. They say stuff like "It's boring," "Humpday Wednesday," "I can't," "It's too hard." Most of their verbal jargon is demotivating. Every time they talk about plans and goals, one word thematically echoes: *but*. "I want to be a rock star, but..." "I want to live debt-free, but..." "I want to travel and see the world, but..." In order for their butts to move in the right direction, they fail to realize the *but* has got to be taken out of the equation.

The Environment

Believers dwell in environments where their gift can thrive. They understand trees grow tall in places of both rain and sunshine, so take them to the everglades, baby. Believers want some Florida heat. Writers spend time with one another. Singers find the same room. Millionaire executives magnetize toward one another. Believers understand it's paramount for the conditions to be right for their gift's growth. They go to conferences, seminars, book signings, workshops, events, shows, meetups, meet and greets, concerts, parades, and wherever else their ambitions can draw power from.

On the other hand, nonbelievers stay at home, watching reruns of reality TV. They migrate where the sun doesn't shine over their gift. Unfortunately, those who are winning big in the areas of their gift are seen as enemies to the nonbeliever. They think and ask themselves, "Why dare solicit advice, give a compliment, or ask for a meeting?" They would much rather stay cooped up at home as their dreams fade away. Nonbelievers don't see the good soil, fertilizer, rain, and sunshine of being in the right place at the right time, so they settle anywhere, even if it means going nowhere.

The Delete Button

Believers constantly delete the unnecessary out of life. The Delete button is a favorite on the keyboard. It signifies power. Eliminate the extra. Precision. Do more with less. If it does not pertain to their gift, passions, and pursuits, then believers do not hesitate in giving it the ax. I don't know much rap music or even listen to it, but O.T. Genasis hit the nail on the head when he said, "You need to cut it!" Believers monitor actions, quite routinely, because they know everyone is subject to weapons of mass distraction, which pose a threat to those soaring high. They delete bad habits, delete fake friends, delete songs off the playlist that sound good but are bad for their spirit.

On the other hand, nonbelievers have a doctorate in addition. They add and add and add. Taking on more of the trivial is okay by their standards. Apparently, they have time for everything, time for gorging on fantasy football and the Home Shopping Network. At one time, the nonbeliever placed limits on indulgences, but now, because the sense of giftlessness is reigning, it's a free-for-all. Self-prescribed freedom of Internet surfing, magazine flipping, late-night-show watching is the plight of the nonbeliever. And how about those obligations that aren't perceived as extracurricular? Serving on the committee, being "homeroom mom," or even being assistant coach on your son's baseball team are some of the ways busyness creeps into the calendar. Out of all the buttons on their keyboard, one is missing in their life: Delete.

The Vision

Believers have a vision in their heart of who they want to become. Their vision is priceless and richer than the shiny gold mines of Africa. Believers safeguard the passions of their hearts, carefully choosing fellow believers to share them with because it's a rarity to trust the unseen. They know the eyes on the face are merely for seeing but the eyes of the heart focus on what is beyond. In their hearts, they envision their show being sold out, performing on international stages, signing their autograph for raving fans, serving an uncountable bevy of people, and giving insane amounts of money to noteworthy charities and causes. Believers typically have a picture board of their future home. On their refrigerators, office walls, and bedroom dresser mirrors, you will find their inspirations. Whether it's visiting exotic vacation spots, owning the fancy homes, leading the nonprofit organization, or starting a family, magazine cutouts and other forms of inspiration are posted around the home to serve as a reminder of what is possible. They feel a strong charge toward their vision. The feeling is more real than real. They can hear, smell, and almost touch their vision. Believers proclaim that the vision is hard-enough evidence to keep them going up!

On the other hand, nonbelievers only see at face value; what is in front of them is what they get. Their vision is limited. Current hardships are harder than normal because they have nothing in their heart suggesting times will get better. Their trajectory of the future is misconstrued by the issues of today. Unfortunately, the cramped apartment, dead-end job, unfaithful partner, and gossipy neighborhood play big roles in their picture. It is hard for the nonbeliever to get past the woes of life. When calamities come, there is little calm or peace because there are no beautiful pictures in a nonbeliever's heart. There is no vision on how one day, life could look completely different for the better. They must have the cold, hard facts. "Shoot it to me straight," they say. There is no room for daydreaming or fantasizing. Therefore, hanging onto life with one finger losing grip, the nonbeliever dangles on a thread while their gifts and dreams are clutched in the other hand. Vision could swoop in, rescue fast, and save the day, but then again, we know how nonbelievers may feel about those odds.

The Kick the Door Down

James Lovell said, "There are people who make things happen, there are people who watch things happen, and there are people who wonder what happened. In order to be successful, you need to be a person who makes things happen." Real believers have what I call a kick-the-door-down moment. It's the time when they are aggressive toward their ambitions. They will not sit idle hoping money will actually grow from trees. They will not pray for the sky to softly drop fame and success on them like an autumn leaf falling from an oak tree. No. They get off their doing nothing and kick the door down. For a believer, staying active and roaming the jungle like a hungry lion is the name of the game.

I recall a local gym that turned down my offer to work as one of their personal trainers. A nice, glossy résumé with my credentials sat on their desks for weeks. As I called a few times to ask for an interview, I got nothing. So my next move was to build it myself. The closed door led to my personal promotion. I instantly became a CEO. The waiting game was over. It was time for me to act. Starting off, I didn't have a door to kick down because my wife and I made the decision to start our fitness business in a public park. We made it happen so well to the point clients were coming out by the dozens and renewing their monthly memberships because of earning jaw-dropping results (while enjoying challenging fitness fun). Talk about kicking down the fitness entrepreneur door in my town; heck, it was bulldozed. A believer believes so much in their heart it becomes very difficult to fold their arms and cross their legs when nothing is happening. Belief forces believers to make things happen!

On the other hand, nonbelievers don't see the door. They don't see the opportunity. If they do happen to see the chance to make it happen, they don't have the fire to kick the door down. They gently knock and forfeit ringing the doorbell to actually get someone's attention. They don't want to make any significant noise in pursuit of their goals. They would much rather receive a handout instead of a hand up. Handouts are more peaceable, and no one is subject to being upset. There is no hostile takeover brewing inside the heart of the nonbeliever. They would rather take a backseat and coast. Where believers understand that some of the best things in life must be taken, nonbelievers will allow an advantageous opportunity to be passersby. They are okay with it passing them up. Believers take phone calls or make phone calls. Nonbelievers wait for the phone to ring. Believers write out their goals and set their plans. Nonbelievers hit the snooze button on their goals and planning, putting it off until tomorrow as if tomorrow were a better day. Tomorrow travels into the distance and becomes a month, year, decade in the life of a nonbeliever. They simply don't use the power of the legs and feet to run up to the door of opportunity and kick the living snot out if it!

The Freedom

Believers see the freedom their gift provides. They don't experience freedom from hard work and dedication. It is not freedom from life getting in the way and presenting adversity or friction. This freedom comes from doing what you know you were born to do. It is the peace of mind knowing you are living on purpose, instead of being like the walking dead. The walking dead are those who are breathing but don't feel alive. There is freedom when serving mankind and operating in a realm that is far bigger than you. There is freedom when you're part of a greater mission and life is more than just simply being about you. Whether it's a heart of service to help stranded puppies or a fearless heart to serve on the front lines of the armed forces, there is freedom from the torment of settling. You can go to bed each night completely exhausted from working your gift and feel completely free because of its executing purpose. You know it matters. You know the stakes are high. You know folks are depending on you, yet you are free.

Nonbelievers have no escape, no outlet. They live in zombie mode. They are tormented by the perpetual cycle of doing and not living. That which is being done does not matter to them, which makes it easy to bail out and check out of life. It's almost an oxymoron type of life because it's easy for nonbelievers but hard as well—

easy because no thought is put into what is next. Life seems pre-planned, prepackaged, canned up, and ready to go: drop the kids off at school, watch the soap operas, pick the kids up from school, then press Repeat. There is no freedom going along to get along. Real freedom is found in your gifts, dreams, purposes, and ambitions; they add color to life.

Why be tormented by black and white when there are HD plasma screens on sale?

Now do you see the difference between one who believes in one's gift versus one who doesn't? Don't simply review the comparisons and contrasts; I want you to rival them, especially the nonbelieving ones. It is perfectly fine to not be entirely on the believing side with all the categories. There are some I have trouble with as well. It is not okay, however, to avoid and resist change. Change is good. Change is growth. Change causes you to believe there is great purpose and destiny inside; believe it to be true.

Fill in the Blanks

1. There are those who believe they are supernaturally gifted and those _____.

2. Believers salivate at the _____, constantly believing they're onto something really big.

3. Positivity _____ of the believer.

4. Believers understand it _____ for the conditions to be right for their gift's maturation.

5. Eliminate the ____.

6. They know the eyes on the face are merely for seeing what is _____ but the eyes of the heart are for seeing what is ____!

7. James Lovell said, "There are people who make things happen, there are people who watch things happen, and there are people who wonder what happened. In order to be successful, you need to be a person who _____.

8. There is freedom from the torment of _____.

Chapter Challenge

Be brutally honest with yourself regarding my question, which category do you fall in: believer or nonbeliever?

Given each one of us can be better and stronger as it relates to our belief system, which one out of the seven do you need to commit the most work to refining: the investment, the language, the environment, the Delete button, the vision, the kick the door down, or the freedom?

Chapter 18

AMAZING GRACE

Amazing grace, how sweet the sound
That saved a wretch like me
I once was lost, but now am found
Was blind, but now I see.

—John Newton

Grace is easily one of my favorite words. Grace is far too deep to explain in a chapter, a book, or even a lifetime, but I will try to break it down for you. Grace is an experience. By definition, it is the free, unmerited favor of God. You cannot earn grace. Grace is given. You cannot buy grace off some shelf in a hardware store. Grace comes freely. I struggle to understand why a powerful gift given by God would cost me nothing. Why does something so sacred and precious, something you and I benefit from so much, have no price tag attached to it? Why can't a sacrifice be made as a form of exchange? Business 101 teaches us: You get what you pay for. Do not complain about dirt-cheap shoes you wore a hole into because you get what you pay for.

It's simple. If I want the fastest car on the planet, with heated bucket seats, an electric sliding sunroof top, metallic paint job, and sparkling rims, then I have to pay handsomely for it. Even if I am filthy rich and money is not an issue, to ride in this type of luxurious car will cost me cash, and lots of it. This is a fair exchange by most people's standards. Despite having lots of greenbacks, the wealthy still have to give them up to get what they want. I absolutely love entrepreneurship, and a lesson learned in my experiences is quite simple: the more one is willing to pay, the more one gets. The bells, whistles, special features, and ridiculous amenities always have a big sticker price. You get what you pay for.

However, grace does not work like that. It doesn't work like that at all, actually. Grace is the total opposite—so opposite and counterintuitive it can be hard to both understand and accept. Grace is unmerited. This means you and I don't deserve it. No matter how good we think we are, no matter how great people think we are, when grace appears in our life, we simply don't deserve it.

In the spirit of competition, namely track and field, whoever runs the fastest gets the prize. Grace doesn't judge whether you qualify or not. It does not equate or factor in your efforts. You cannot justify being a recipient of grace. Grace is simply God being unreasonably good and choosing to bless both you and me. The apostle Paul said, "By the grace of God, I am what I am, and his grace toward me was not in vain. On the contrary I worked harder than any of them, though it was not I, but the grace of God that is with me" (1 Corinthians 15:10).

Paul was saying a lot here, but not enough. He left a great deal unspoken, so allow me to fill in the gaps. Paul was acknowledging the sum total of his life experiences, which shaped him into who he was. He considered himself more than any other Christian. He worked harder, was more frequently thrown in prison, took more beatings, and even escaped death time and time again for the sake of the gospel. The Paul you see in 1 Corinthians 15:10 is the same one who received 195 (yes, almost 200) lashes from the Jews. Hit with rods, nearly crushed with stones, shipwrecked, spent days out in the open sea, hungry, thirsty, naked, cold, marred with many sleepless nights described the lifestyle of Paul (see 2 Corinthians 11:23–28).

Yet by the grace of God, he withstood the fiery fires of life and proclaimed unmerited favor toward him. No kidding! After having endured such tumultuous times, Paul still wrote most of the New Testament in the Holy Bible. He gave everything possible to the cause of utilizing his afforded grace. He didn't give up, didn't throw in the towel, didn't wipe his hands clean of the mission, even though he nearly lost his life several times. How in the world did he survive the thunderstorms and accomplish such great feats? Grace, my friend.

Can you boldly say like Paul "And His grace toward me was not in vain?" God is showing you favor right now as you take breath after breath, as your heartbeat thumps routinely. He's also inspiring your heart as you intriguingly read about the power of grace right now. When you know God is for you and He has issued special favor, nothing can stop you. We are stronger than measureable with Him.

"If God be for us, then who can be against us" (Romans 8:31). When the Creator of the universe is on your side, you can't even stop you!

Do you notice how Paul is a wee bit braggadocio with his words? Take a closer look at how he almost corrected himself while speaking about grace. "I work harder than any of them, though it was not I." He, without any uncertain terms, was staking his claim to being the best but then covered it up with a (let me paraphrase) "But wait a minute, it is not me doing the magic here, folks—it's God!'

Be very careful of the pride and haughtiness that makes itself readily available to you while operating in the grace of God. Monitor closely. Learn from Paul and quickly deflect the fascination of you and your gifts back onto the one who graced you in the first place. It is very easy to fall in love with your gift and forget about the Gift Giver. In fact, God will grant you more grace when humility is your forte. "He resists the proud and gives grace to the humble" (James 4:6).

His grace and your gift are a lethal combination. God wants to make sure, as you grow in your supernatural abilities, you remember the Supplier. He doesn't want you to lose your marbles for a second thinking you arrived on your own merits. Remember, grace is unmerited. I know my next few lines may upset you and unnerve you. However, here I go…

Your influence: unmerited. Your success: unmerited. Your peace: unmerited. Your expensive education: unmerited. Your beautiful kids: unmerited. Your three-story house: unmerited. Your sanity in this crazy world: unmerited. The ability to see the beautiful sunrise: unmerited. Walking on your own two feet: unmerited. Freedom: unmerited. Your impressive career: unmerited. The puppy that wags its tail at the sight of you: unmerited. The supportive spouse who absolutely adores you: unmerited. The sweet scent of rain's arrival: unmerited.

When all is said and done, all of it belongs to one rightful owner, whom many may consider generous to a fault, God. Grace is a gift. The talents you have are a gift. Your drive, passions, motives, and ambitions, aligned with the will of God, are a gift. "Every good and perfect gift is from above, coming down from the Father of heavenly lights, who does not change" (James 1:17).

Allow real peace to overtake you while understanding amazing grace. John Newton wrote, "Amazing grace, how sweet the sound."

Yes, grace has a sound.

I didn't know what John meant at first, but through prayer, I now understand. The sound of grace is inescapable. It is everywhere you go. Grace is hearing the autumn leaves whisper in the trees on a brisk, windy day. Grace is your spouse softly speaking into your ear; with her first morning words, she says, "I love you." Grace is listening to the comforter and sheets ruffle as your kids roll over in bed. Grace is the sound of warm running bathwater as it hits the tub. Even if you're deaf and unable to hear with your ears, grace is listening to the Word of God reverberate in the mind goodness like "You're above and not beneath," "You're more than a conqueror," "He will rejoice over you with gladness," "For God so loved the World, that he gave his only Son, that whoever believes in him should not perish but have eternal life" (Deuteronomy 28:13, Romans 8:37–39, Zephaniah 3:17).

Grace has a sweet, sweet sound spread throughout the four corners of the earth. Grace is constantly humming like a bird, constantly around. If you are not alert, you can easily miss it like the beautiful, extravagant landmarks in a hometown overlooked by its natives.

Once you've understood that grace is made ripe for your picking, get ready for instant power. You will be exposed to ridiculous power, the type of power to climb Mount Everest, the type of power to swim from Cuba to Florida, the type of power to run a mile in under four minutes, the type of power to march on Selma, Alabama. Amazing grace! You have no reason to fear, no reason to doubt, no reason to be a skeptic of what the sovereignty of God chooses to freely give away. Oh, how great the wonderful adventures, thrills, and joys that await because of sweet grace.

Fill in the Blanks

1. Grace is the _____ favor of God.

2. It is very easy to fall in love with the gift and _____ about the _____.

3. Amazing grace, how _____ the _____.

4. Grace has a _____.

5. When understanding grace made ripe for your picking, get ready for _____.

Chapter Challenge

Acknowledge the grace granted to you. Utilize it to the fullest extent. Find ways to push yourself beyond the status quo. Read more books, start writing your own novel, serve people more faithfully, change careers for the sake of doing what you've always wanted to do. Grace will appear when you take steps in the right direction. Listen for the sweet sound it makes.

Epilogue

I am so proud of you. You made it to the end of *Born Gifted* and the beginning of your newfound joy of conquering your gift. There is a lot to be said about your resiliency. Thank you for sticking it out with me.

You learned a lot about yourself, right? Now is a good time to combat any fear trying to seep into your spirit due to what you have learned. Whispers of coming failures will try to haunt you. Tell them to shut up! Remember, failure is not death, nor is it you. Zig Ziglar said, "Failure is an event, not a person." Take the lessons learned in the pursuit of mastering your gift and keep seeing the big picture bigger as it relates to your future. The future looks gigantic for you. I know you feel it. I do too.

Allow me to encourage you to revisit the "Fill in the Blanks" and "Chapter Challenges." Let the concepts and principles I taught you cement deeply into your heart and mind. You, my friend, are a brand-new person already. Give yourself permission to feel amazing about it.

You now understand your gift is designed to zap the boredom out of life. You have not tapped out on your potential.

The fun part is realizing your gift comes natural to you.

This gift was freely and willingly given to you by God. He doesn't want it back either. He gave richly, with no regrets.

Now everyone must stand on guard for your talent advisory alert as you broadcast loudly who you are and what you were born to do.

In times of trouble, uncertainty, and even great struggle, reading the context clues from your past or present will help you strive toward making a difference. You have come to understand that the place of tremendous pain and hardship is also the place of opportunity and growth. So don't take the hardships too hard.

This friction and adversity give you an advantage.

As you develop your greatness, acknowledge that greatness takes time. Michael Jordan did not start off as Air Jordan. In fact, he was cut from his high school basketball team. It takes a lifetime to become an overnight success. Keep coming back, again and again, because you are learning how to become an expert who is second to none.

When cheers and admiration begin to flood, because you have mastered your craft, keep good character a priority. Don't let the applause go to your head. Man-made pedestals are dangerous. Humbly bow, point to the sky, move off the stage, and remember God is more enamored with your character than your gift.

Because your character and gift are a dynamic duo, you will have an issue quitting vain pursuits. You will feel the demand to want to please everyone.

Quitting, however, is a vital part of the process and your progress. Be a guru of the one thing. It's not all about what you start but what you stop that will lead to your success. Recognize what is yours and what belongs to someone else.

Your gift is too big to lose focus. Think of the heaven on earth by spending the majority of your awake time living out your passions, dreams, and ambitions. Your gift is so gigantic the trivial must move over.

Why? Because your gift's mission is to not only bless you but also profoundly touch and serve other people; it deserves your undivided attention. God has assigned you to people who need both you and your gift.

Winning the war zone in the mind in order to carry out your assignment is key. A mind is a terrible thing to waste; keep it elevated by thinking of the praiseworthy—the sunshine, the laughter of kids, the special holidays coming up.

Work your gift. To thine craft be true. There is nothing to replace good old-fashioned hard work and dedication as you ascend.

You have creative juices flowing to make your gift stand out among others. Make creativity your daily multivitamin. I am willing to bet, if you thought long and hard enough, a new idea will come right now. This will help you use your gift in a brand-new way.

Then after having done all this, if brutal reminders of the past come to haunt you, concentrate on the gift of restoration. God is a Restorer. Believe that everything lost or taken will be given back to you, "pressed down, shaken together, and running over" (Luke 6:38).

It boils down to what you believe: Choose to believe you are God's chosen. Your attributes are meant to set the world on fire. Believers speak with intentionality; they spend their money differently and have acute vision.

Yes, you fall within the believer category.

You have amazing grace on your side.

You have a supernatural power in you.

And you use it to accelerate and excel.

Absolutely, you were born gifted!

Your Personal Invitation

Allow me to be clear.

If at any point during Born Gifted, you said, "Nisan, your story sounds great, but I'm not you," then we must stay connected.

If while reading this book, countless dark and gloomy thoughts plagued your mind about the shortcomings of your past only to project your future failure and demise, then we must stay connected.

If there were internal battles waged to even believe a single word I wrote, then again, we must stay connected.

God gifted me to write Born Gifted specifically for you.

Let's get one thing correct: I'm no more special than you.

We both bleed red.

We both need water to survive.

We both put our pants on one leg at a time.

If I'm able to overcome doubt, self-limiting beliefs, fear, poverty, public disgrace and mockery, then so can you.

If the transformation story of ashes to beauty happened for me, then it can happen for you.

We cannot lose with the power of God on our side.

I wish this book were the perfect remedy and answer for everything you need, but both you and I know, you need much more than my written words.

Working alongside highly motivated, "everyday" people within the Born Gifted Community will prove to be monumental toward your growth and progress as well.

Imagine having the social accountability and camaraderie of the BGC in addition to my proven, time-tested coaching strategies of success.

This opportunity is key to your upgrade given life is now forced to test you because of completing Born Gifted.

That's right! The battle has just begun.

Whether it be mentally, emotionally, spiritually, or physically, life will attempt to press into you harder due to what you have learned here.

Now that you have been fairly forewarned, are you prepared to go to the next level?

Are you equipped to go the distance with your gift despite the difficulties of life? How can you ensure victory on every front?

By taking action and joining my private on-line group coaching program, I am extremely confident you will soar to higher heights.

I'm gifted to personally coach you on how to unpack the gifts inside you for supernatural success. I'm gifted to help you win big.

So, I would be remiss to end Born Gifted without personally inviting you to join my private on-line group coaching program.

We must stay connected. Go to www.nisantrotter.com/invitation or email me at nisanrpm@nisantrotter.com to learn more about The Born Gifted Community.

I will see you there!

Chapter 2 Answer Key:
1. Detached
2. Respecter, favoritism
3. Giftless

Chapter 3 Answer Key:
1. Actual clues
2. Immeasurable capabilities
3. Hardwired, touched

Chapter 4 Answer Key:
1. Growth strategy
2. Irrevocable
3. Need each other to survive

Chapter 5 Answer Key:
1. Powerful beyond measure
2. Faith, purchase
3. Reintroduce, you

Chapter 6 Answer Key:
1. Stripped of our identity
2. Disqualify
3. Shine the most

Chapter 7 Answer Key:
1. Adversity, friction
2. The best at your gift
3. Distractions
4. Perfect, always

Chapter 8 Answer Key:
1. Time
2. Control
3. Fear, anxiety, negativity, jealousy, focus

Chapter 9 Answer Key:
1. Character
2. Search
3. With you as His child

Chapter 10 Answer Key:
1. Quitting
2. Time
3. Expired, opportunity

Chapter 11 Answer Key:
1. What they love to do
2. Consistent and concerted effort, wearing yourself out

Chapter 12 Answer Key:
1. Upline, sideline, downline
2. Teacher, student
3. Pearls

Chapter 13 Answer Key:
1. Own life
2. Toxic thoughts
3. Mind-set

Chapter 14 Answer Key:
1. Massive action
2. Right
3. Average, phenomenal
4. Big, heavy

Chapter 15 Answer Key:
1. Conditioned, regular
2. How to use your gift
3. Natural

Chapter 16 Answer Key:
1. Comeback
2. To bring back

Chapter 17 Answer Key:
1. Who do not
2. ROI - Return On Investment
3. Rolls off the tongue
4. Paramount
5. Extra
6. In front of you, beyond you
7. Make things happen
8. Settling

Chapter 18 Answer Key:
1. Unmerited
2. Forget, Gift Giver
3. Sweet, sound
4. Sound
5. Instant power

Growing up in the backwoods of Silverhill, Alabama, Nisan's humble beginnings spurred on incredible ambition. After witnessing his mother feverishly work minimum-wage jobs to barely scrape by, he knew a better life meant ruthlessly applying himself to school and sports.

His hard work had proved extremely valuable in earning a football scholarship to one of the nation's top academic institutions, Bucknell University. Gifted with a massive work ethic, stirring leadership, and infectious speaking skills, Trotter's teammates voted him Most Inspirational Player of the Year. He was also awarded the university's first ever Diversity Achiever Award because of being able to compassionately connect with any undergraduate.

As a first-generation college graduate, Nisan took a leap of faith by leaving a job with comfortable pay to pursue his dreams of becoming a fitness entrepreneur. From starting grass roots at the local outdoor public park to now having a stand-alone studio, Trotter's establishment (co-owned by his wife) is one of the most successful fitness outlets in the Greater Susquehanna Valley of Central Pennsylvania. In fact, his success garnered national and international attention en route to winning the 2015 Fitness Business Summit Personal Trainer of the Year Award.

Nisan is now a highly sought-after motivational speaker. He's presented across the nation as the Fitness Preacher. *Extremely uplifting* and *unbelievably good* are only a few words that describe his speaking style. His life's stories are cunningly crafted to empower and inspire. He's a living witness that your gift(s) can take you anywhere. Whether it's private coaching, presenting before business executives, or arousing an auditorium full of high school students, Trotter loves helping everyone discover they have a supernatural gifting in them to accelerate and excel.

He's been madly in love with his beautiful bride, Yorelis, for nearly a decade, and he's on a nonstop cheek-kissing mission with his two little boys, Onesimus and Osias!

CPSIA information can be obtained
at www.ICGtesting.com
Printed in the USA
LVHW041607010419
612558LV00003B/485/P